Simple Flowers Large Print Coloring Book

This Coloring book belongs to:

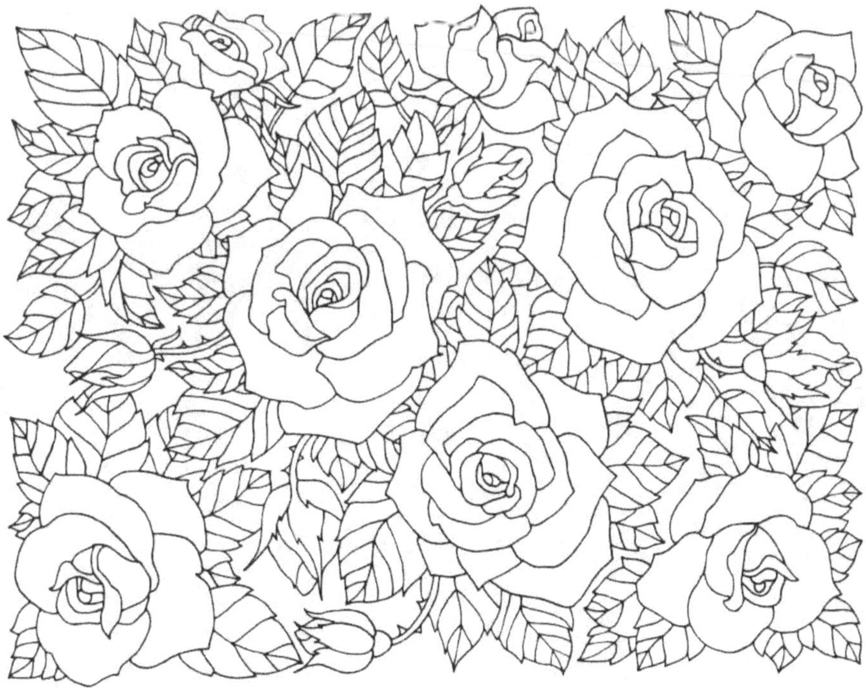

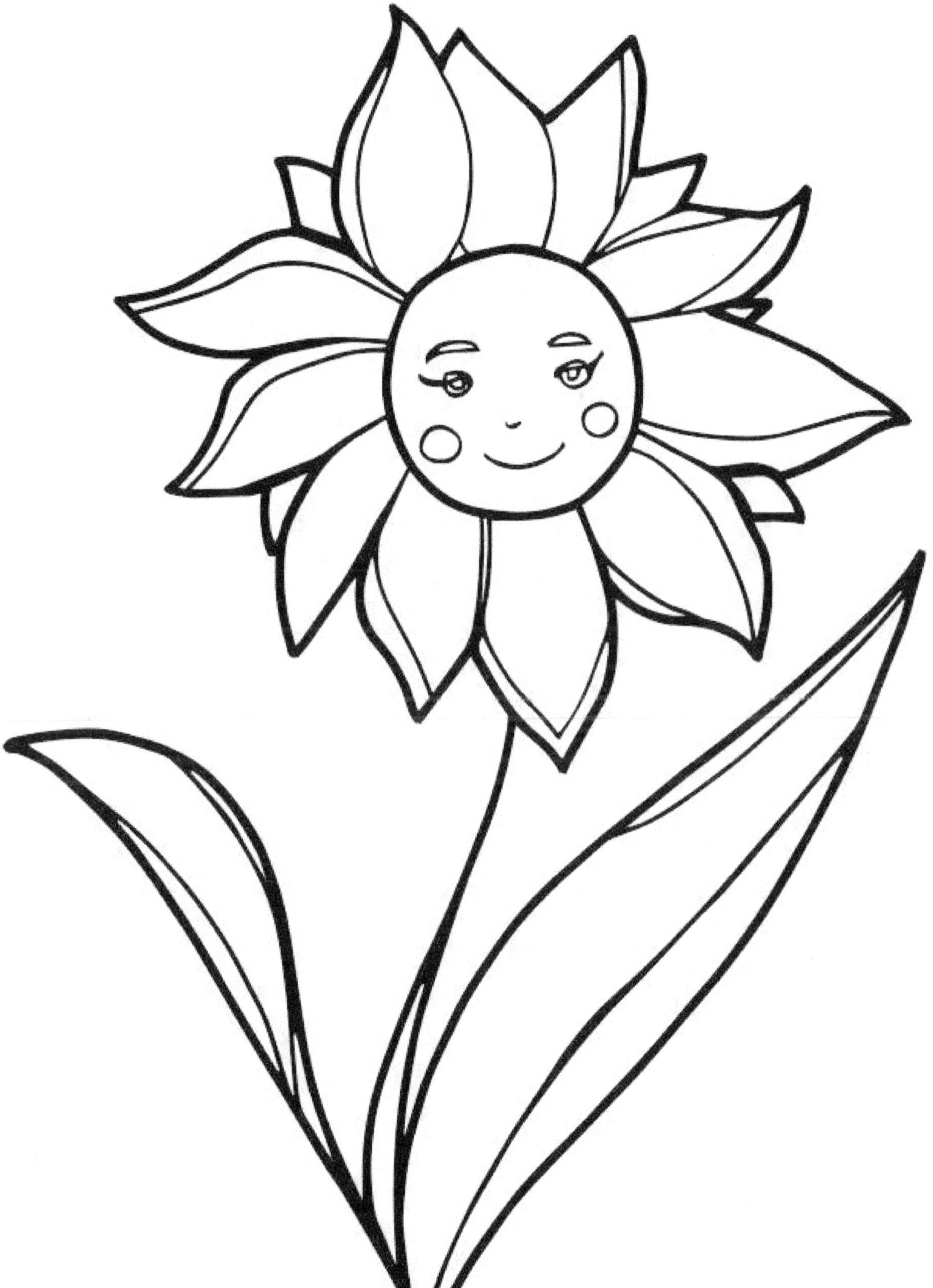

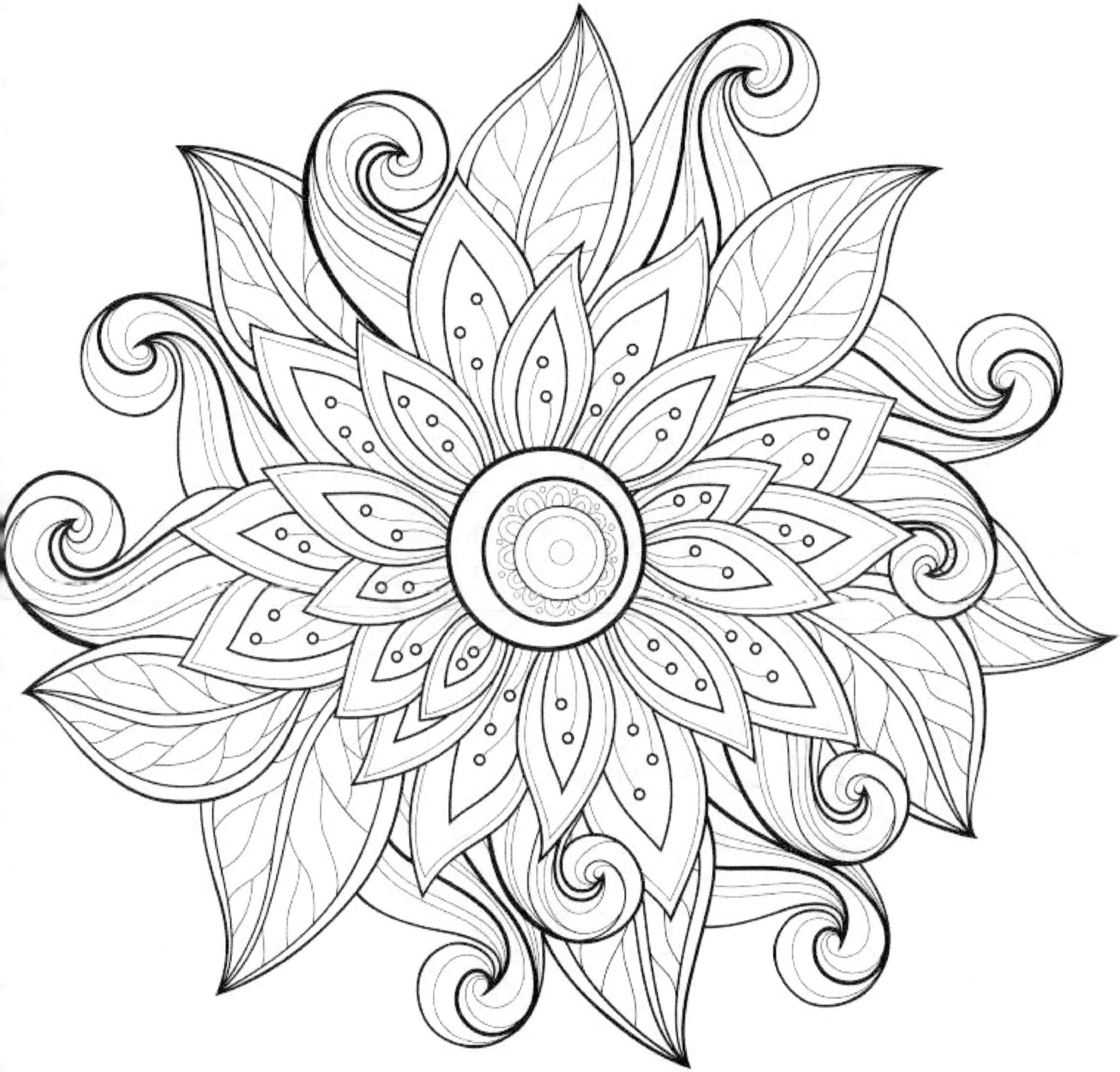

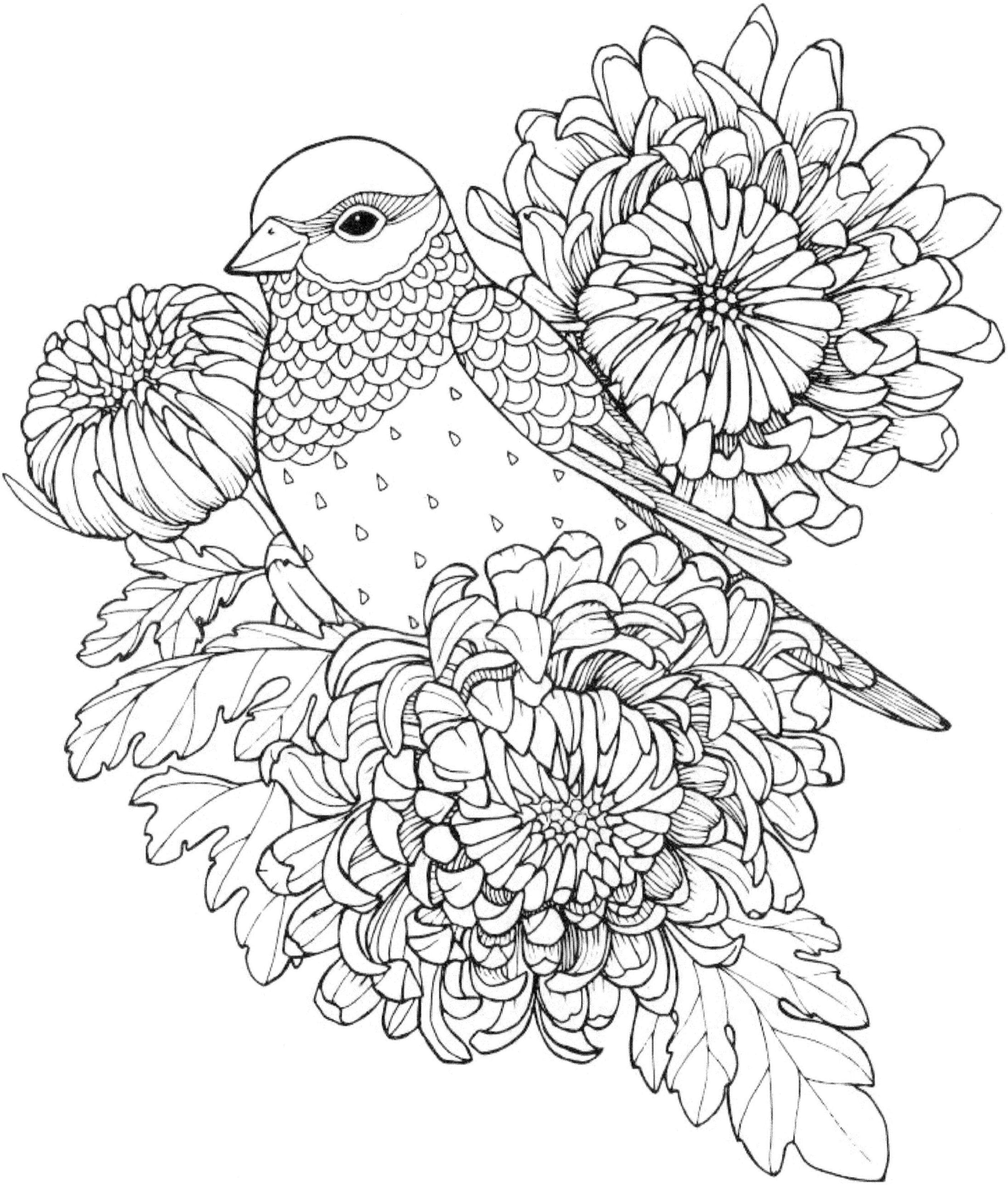

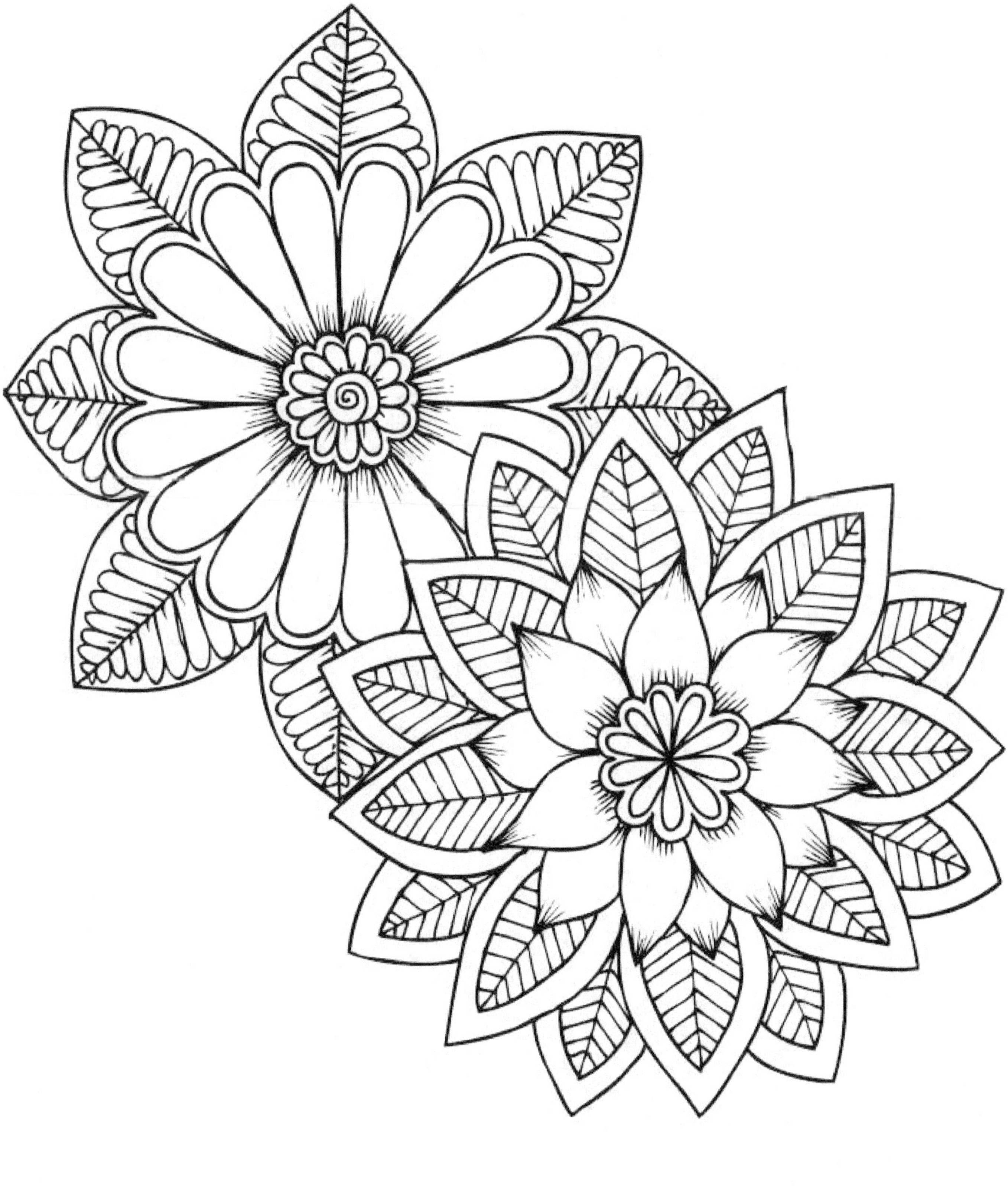

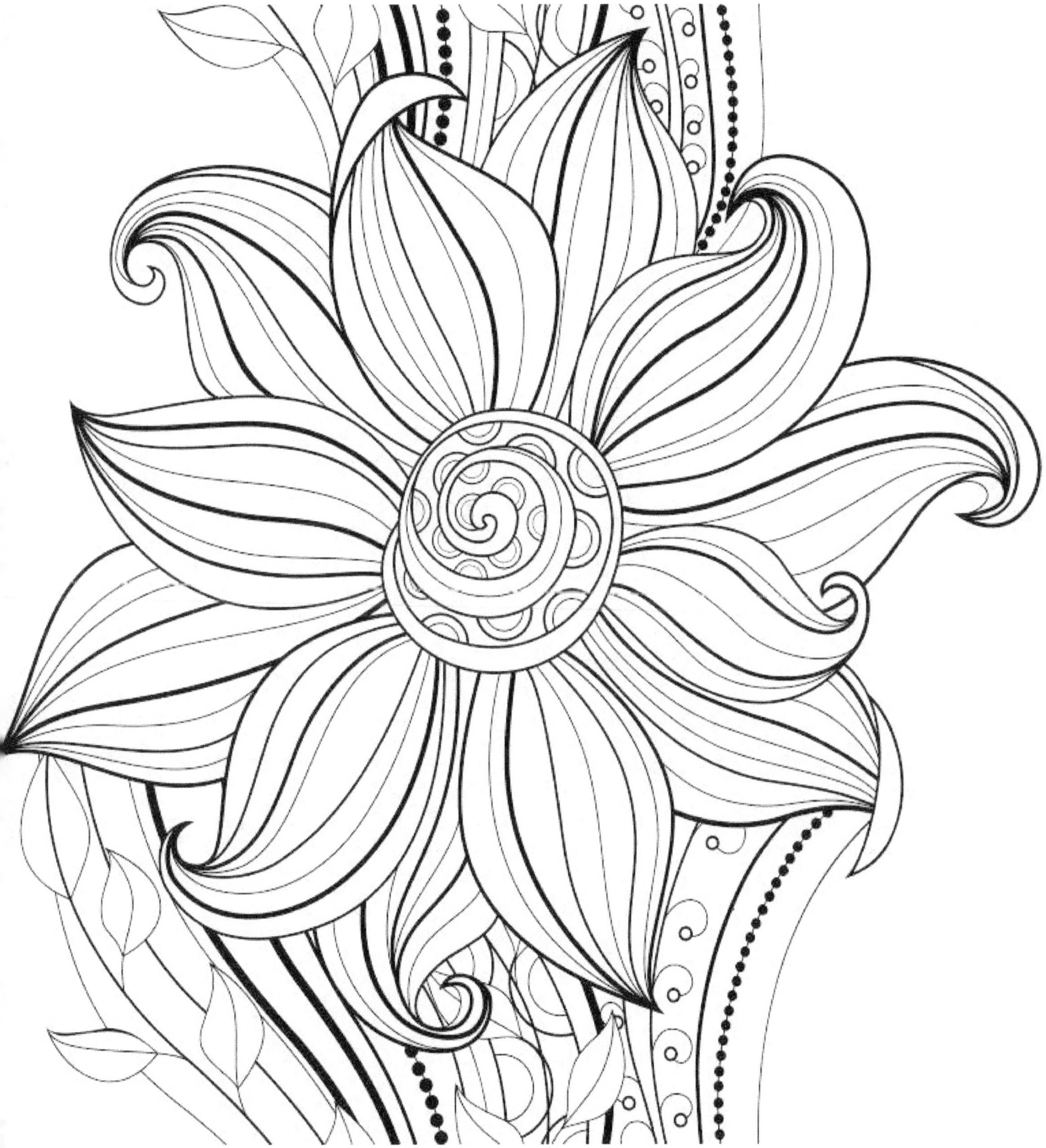

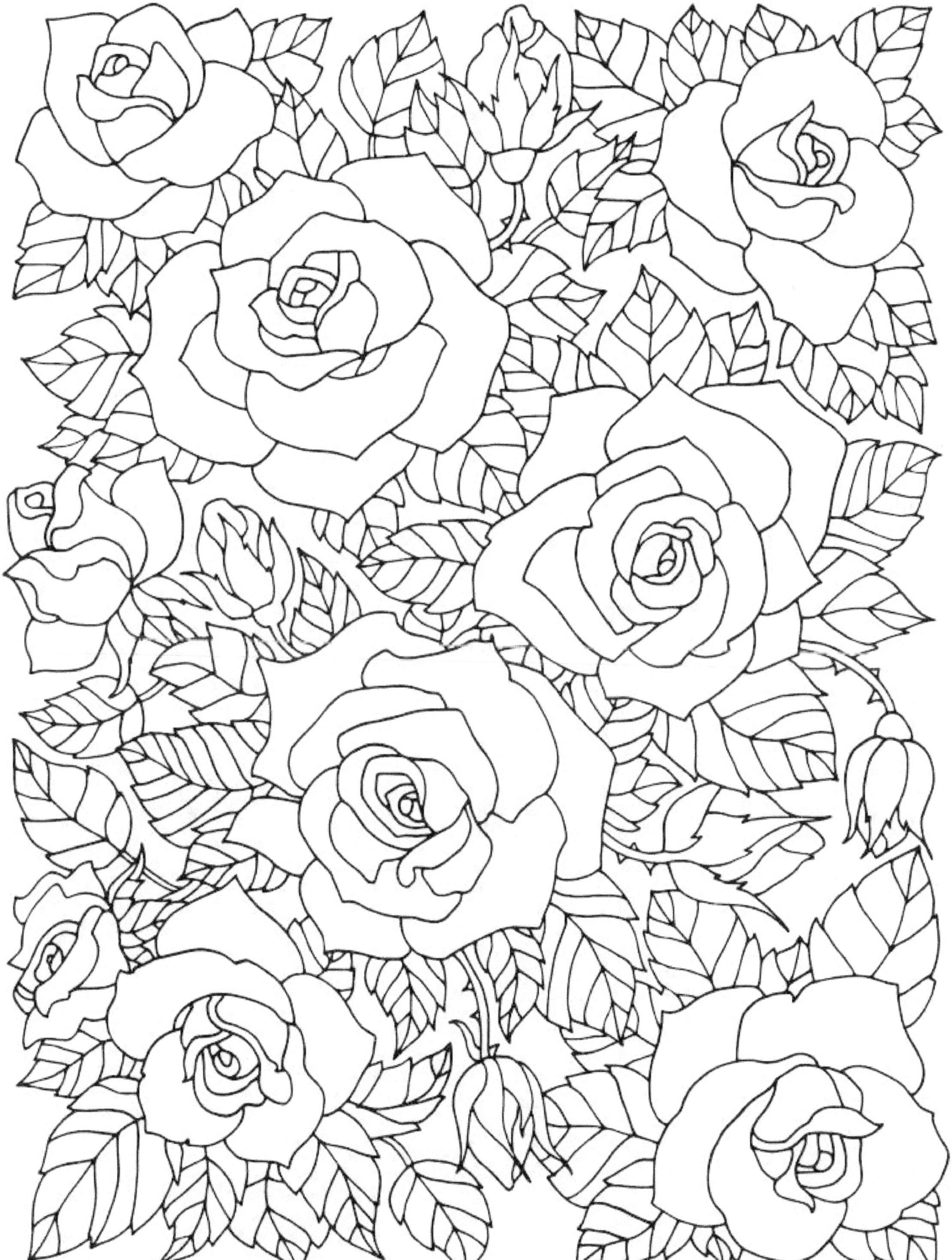

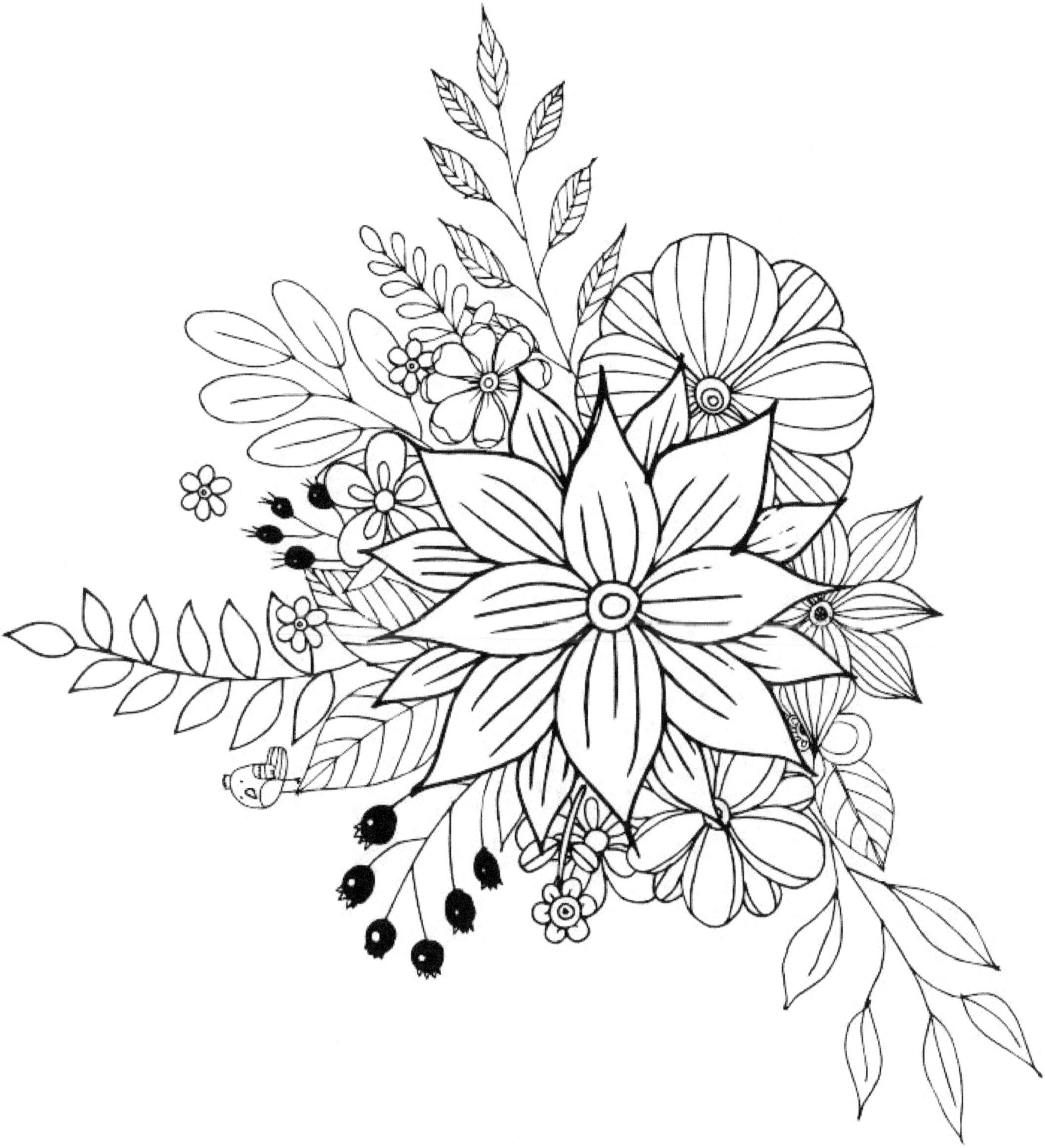

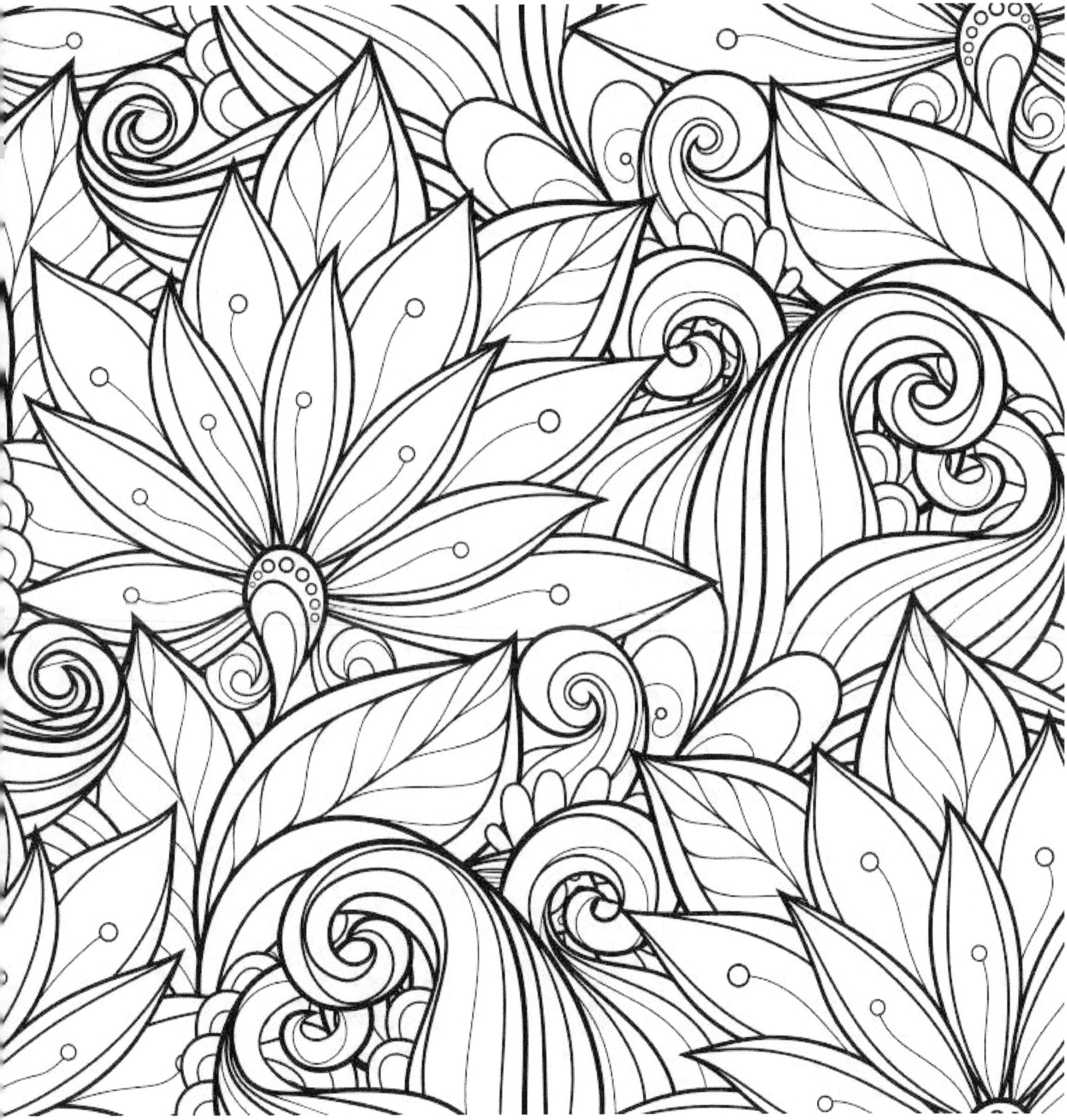

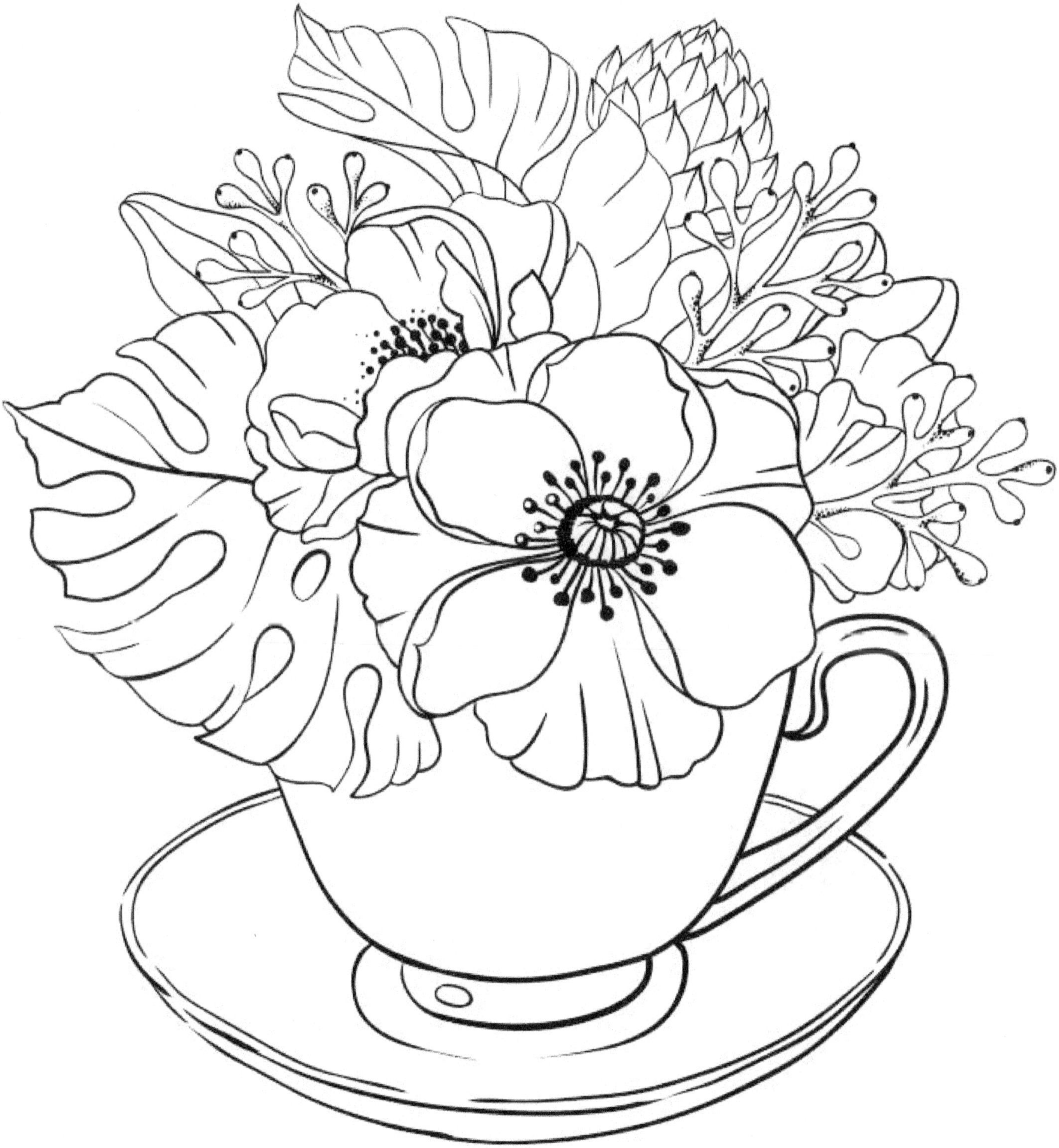

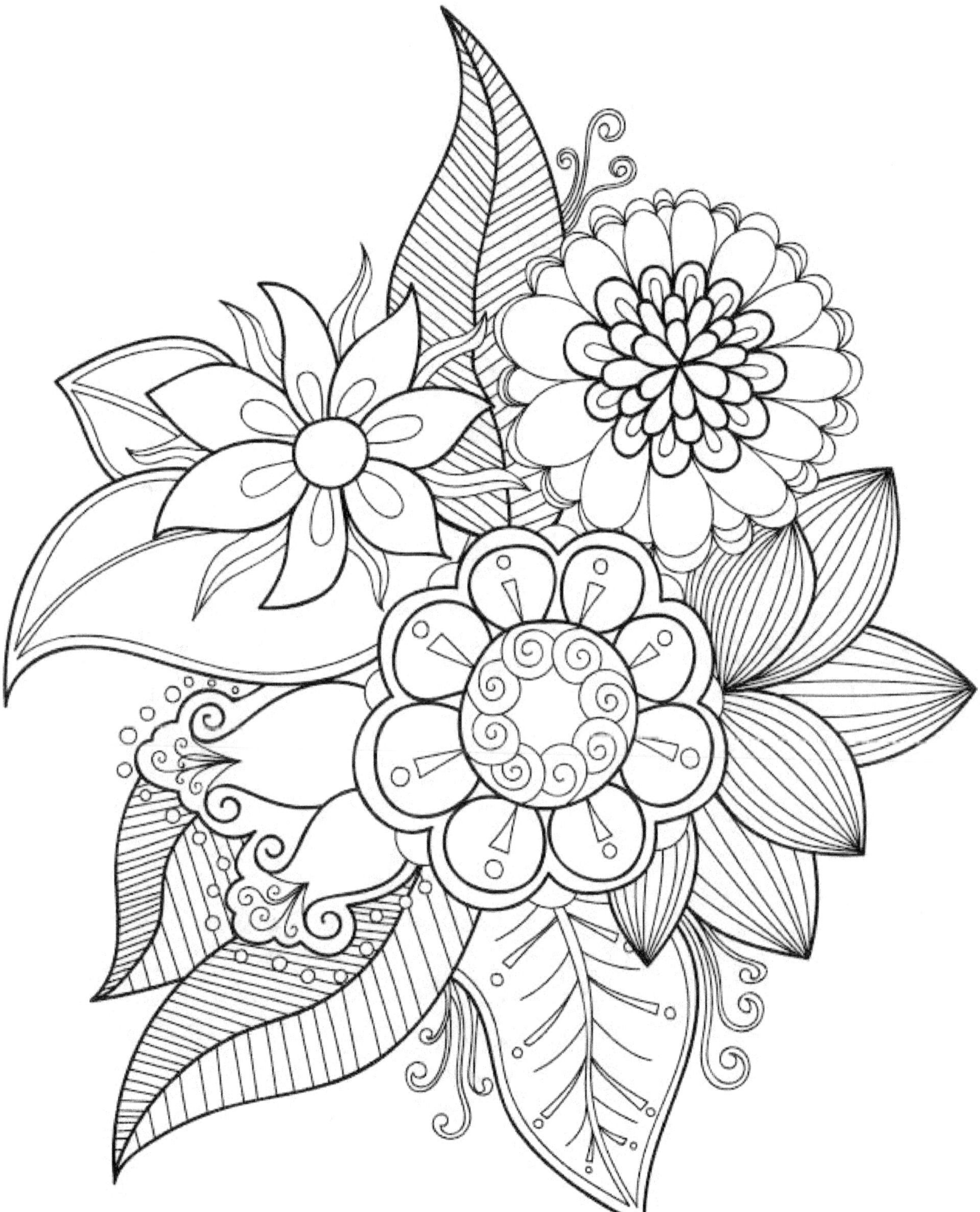

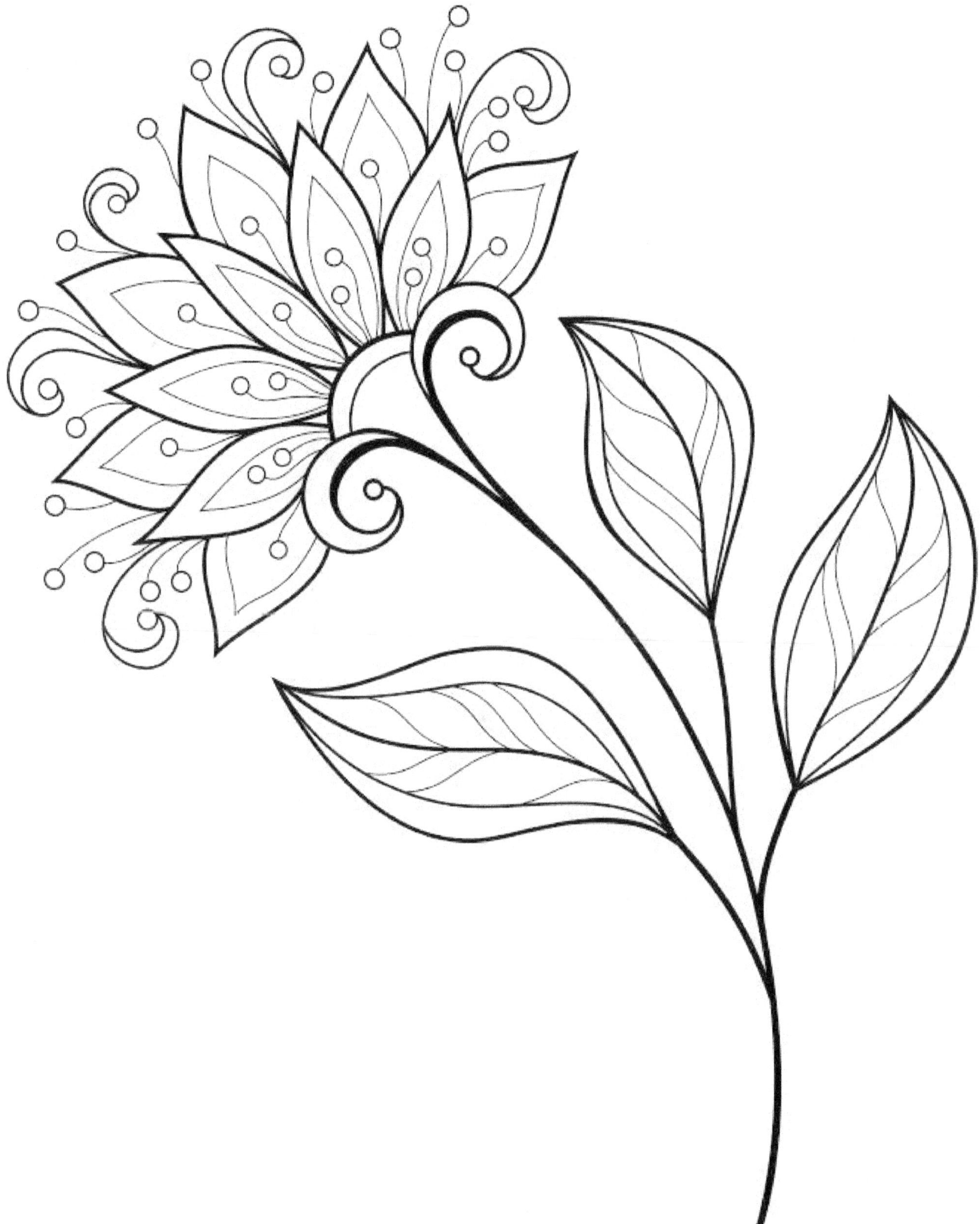

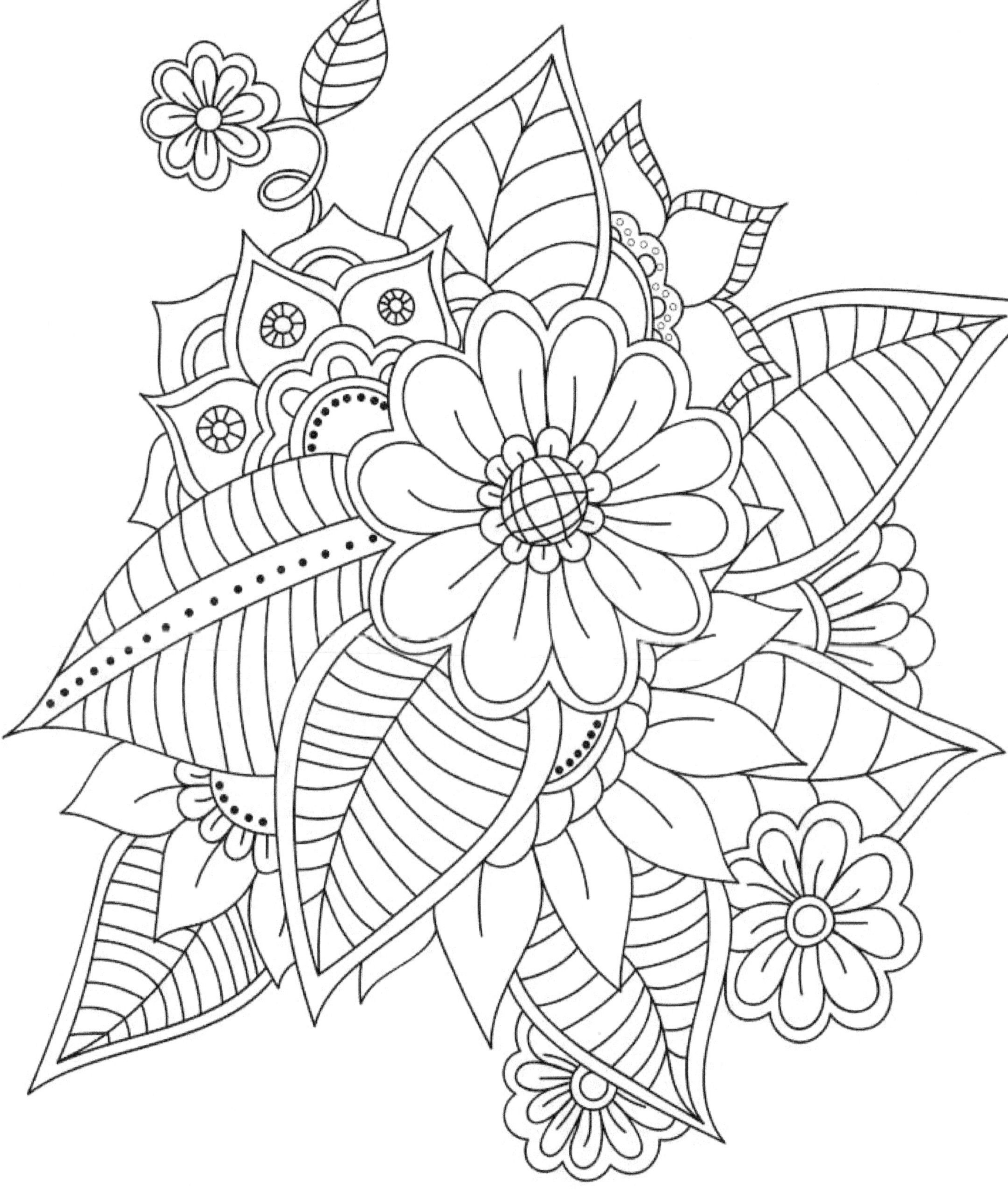

Surprise Bonus Dog Breeds and Beautiful Sea Turtles Coloring Pages!

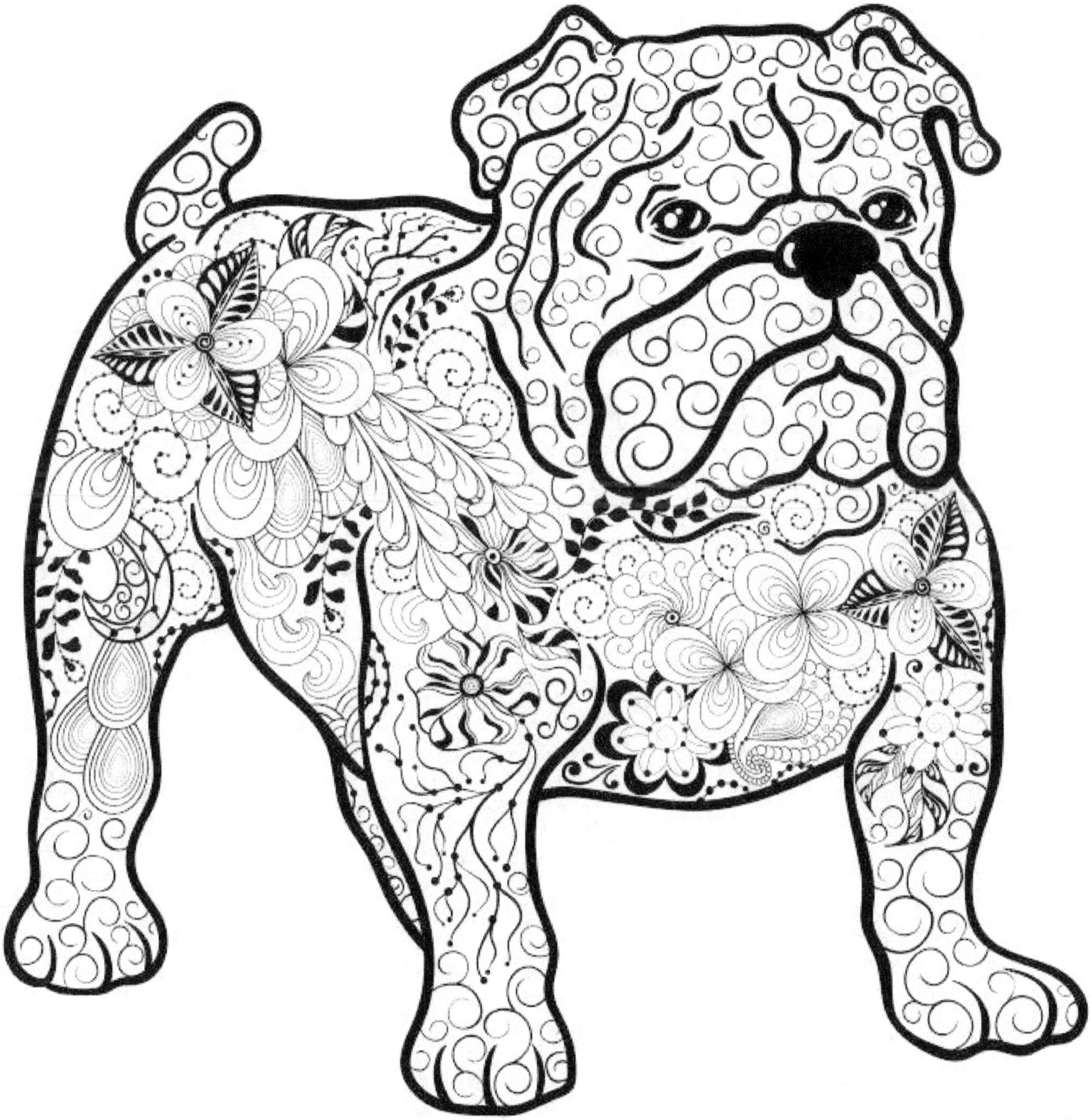

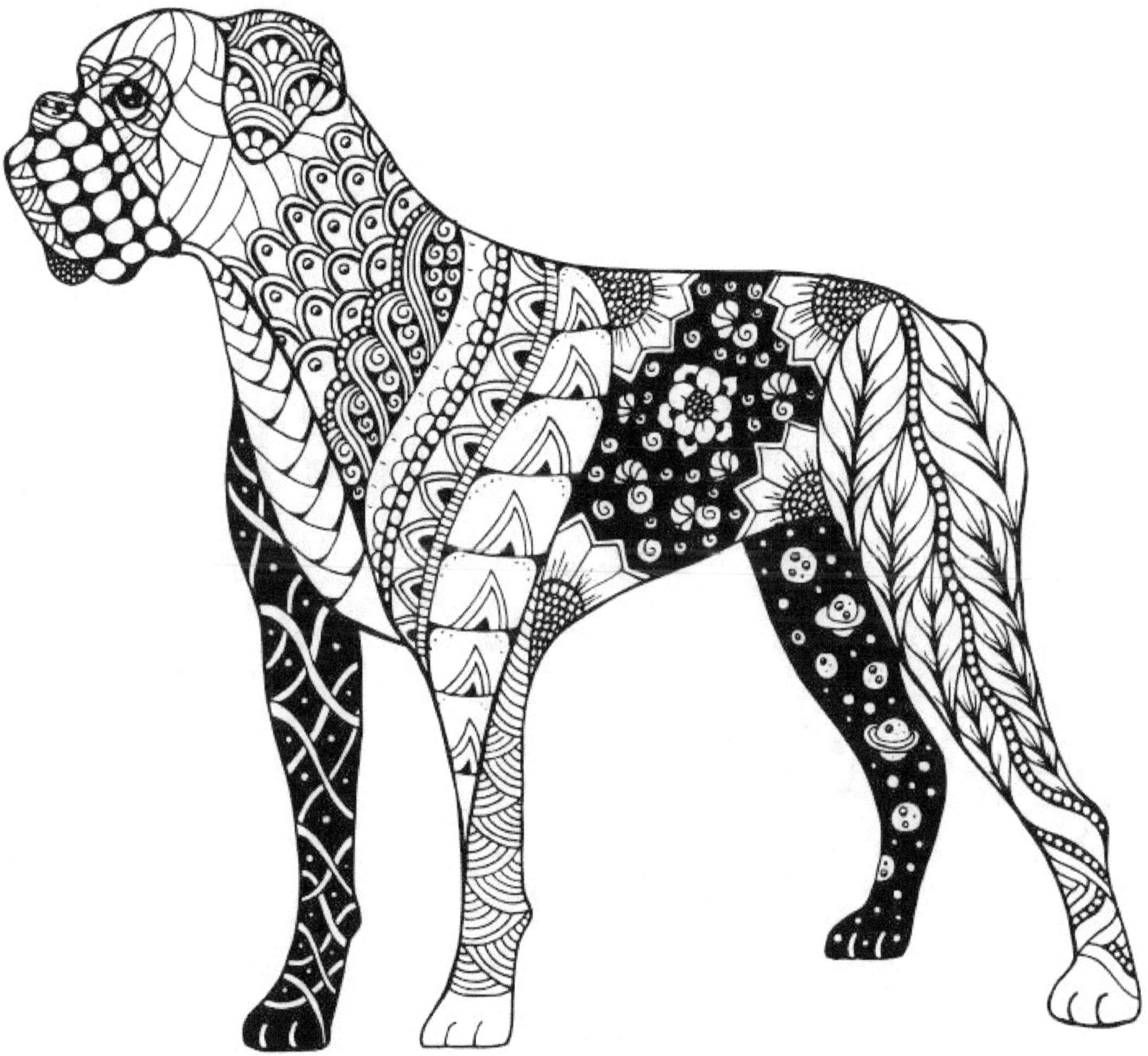

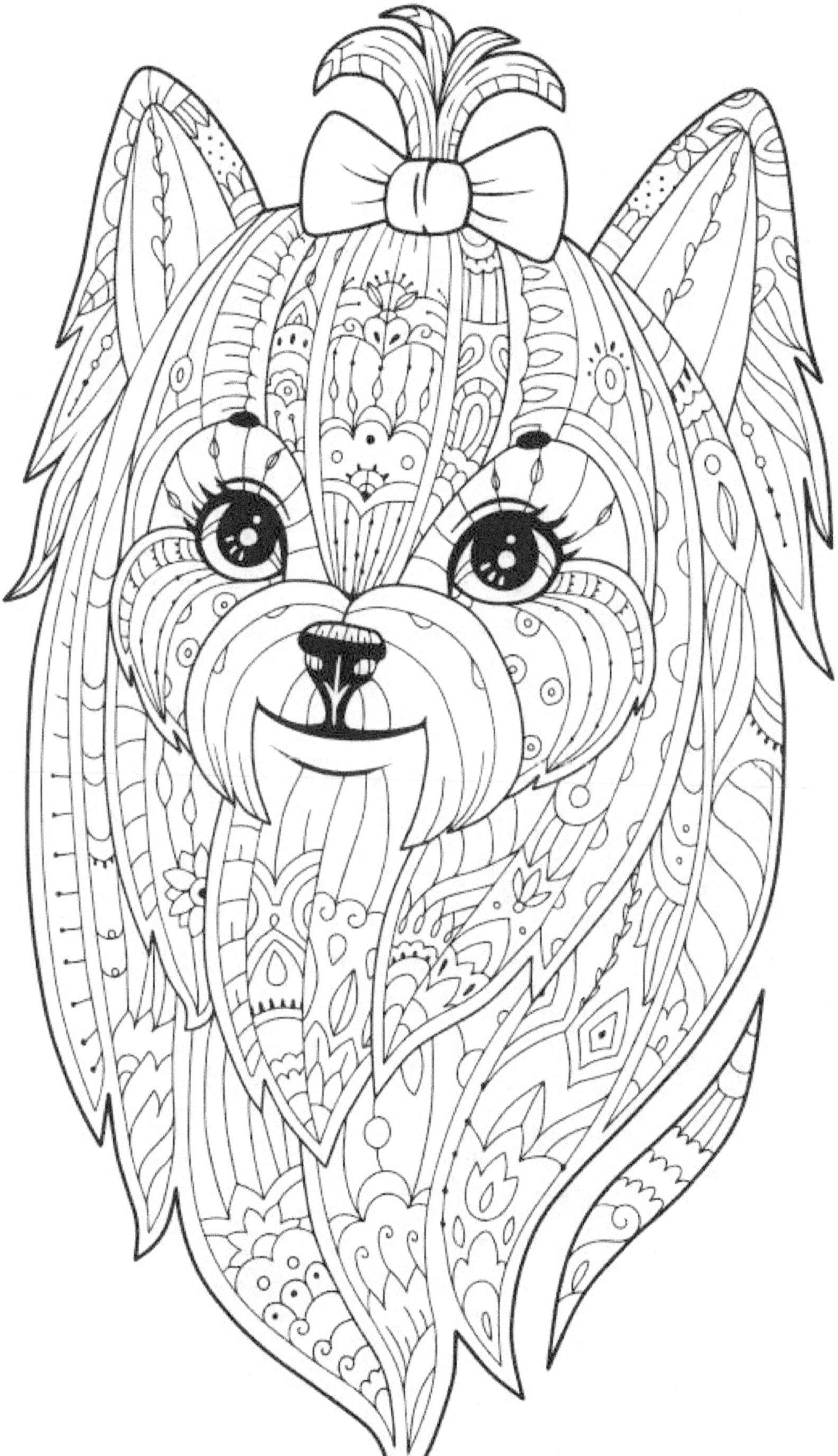

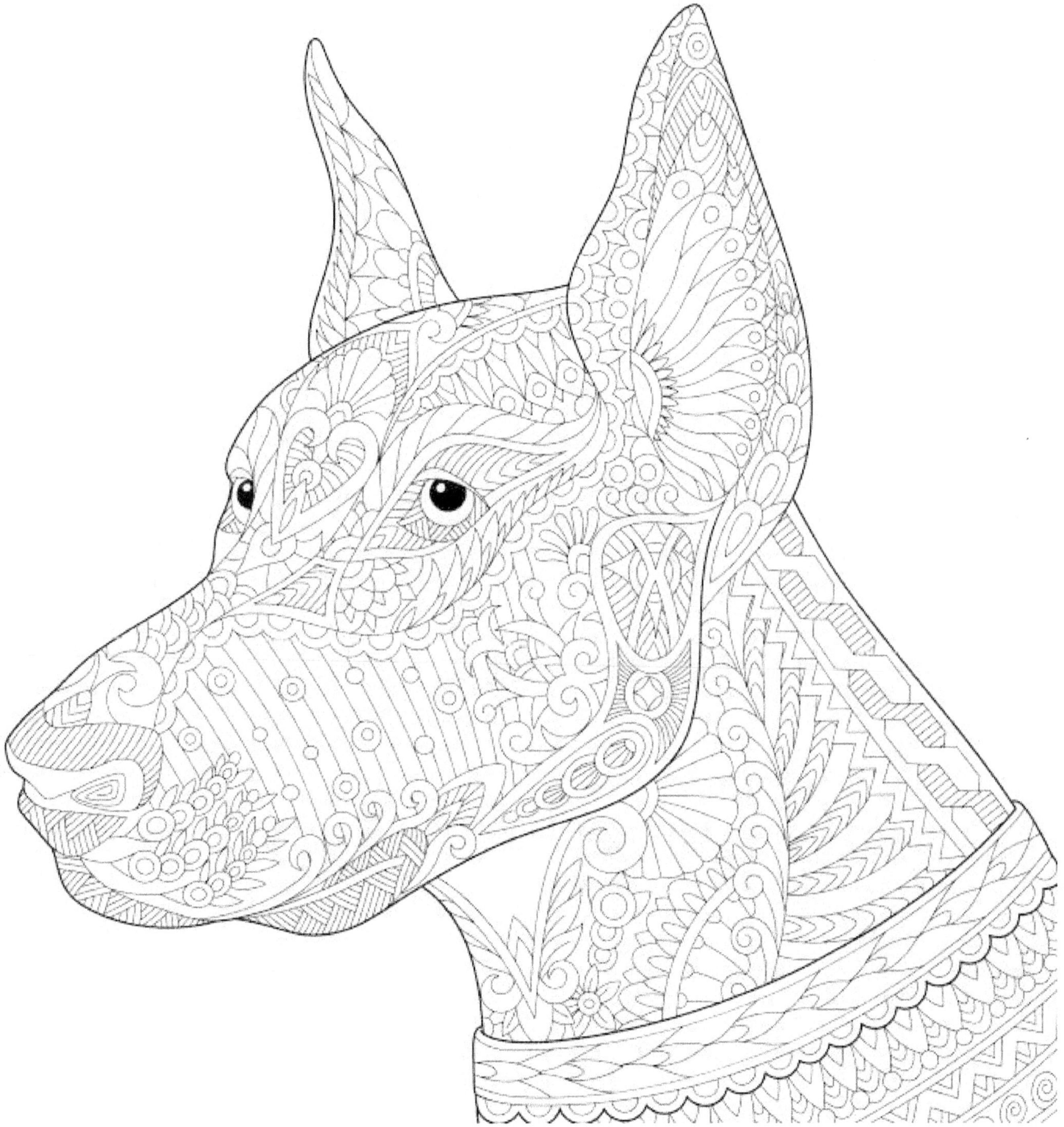

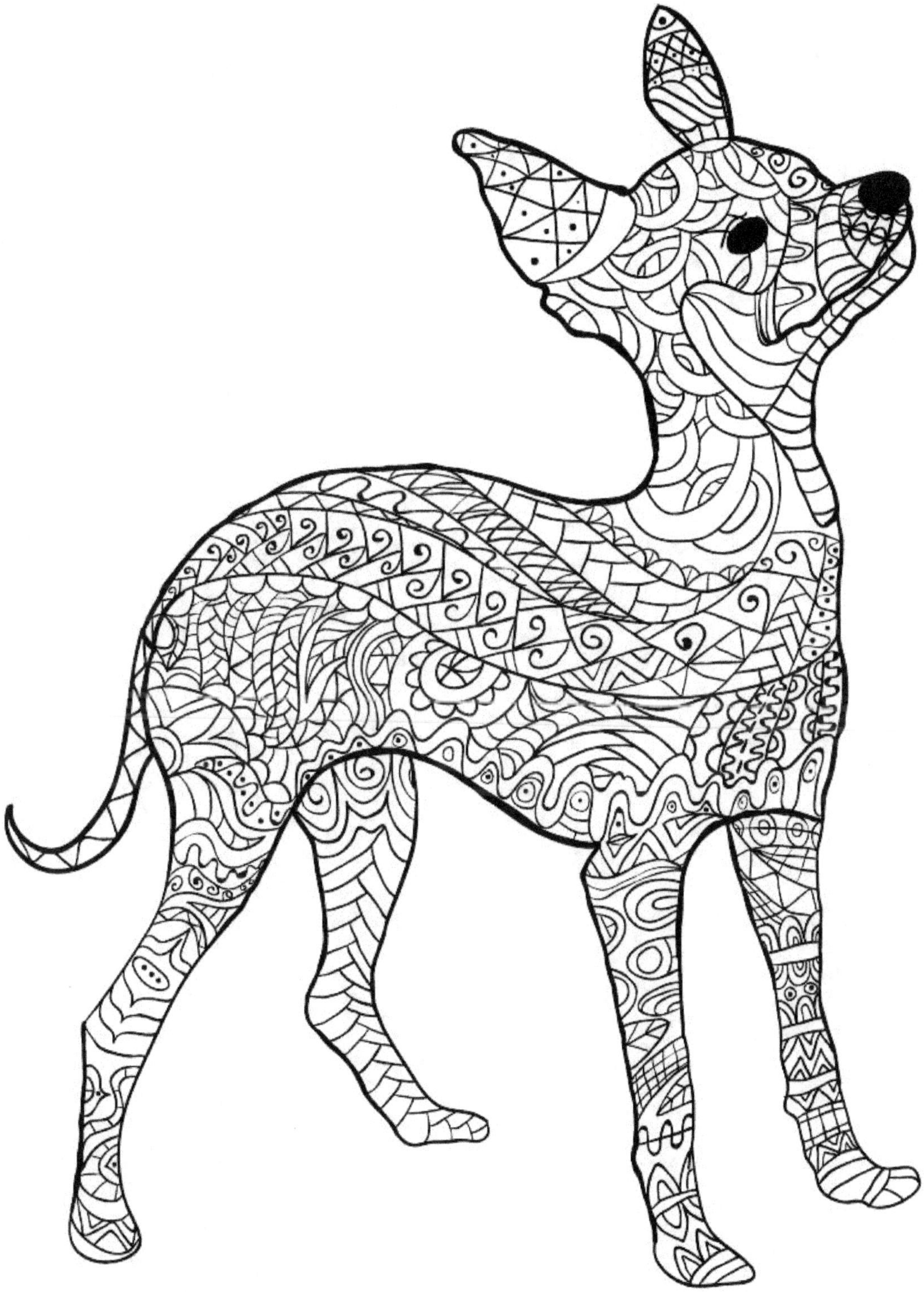

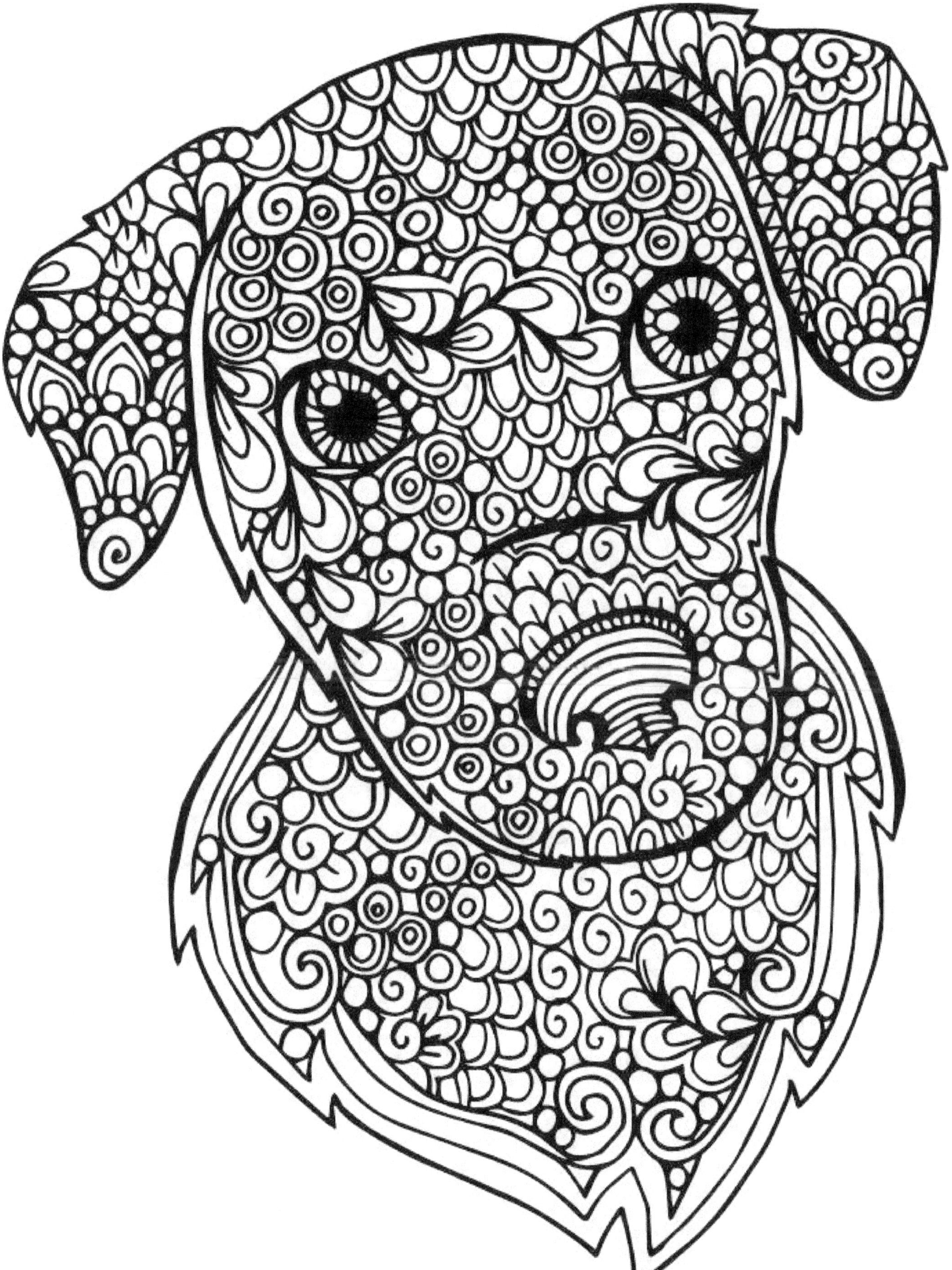

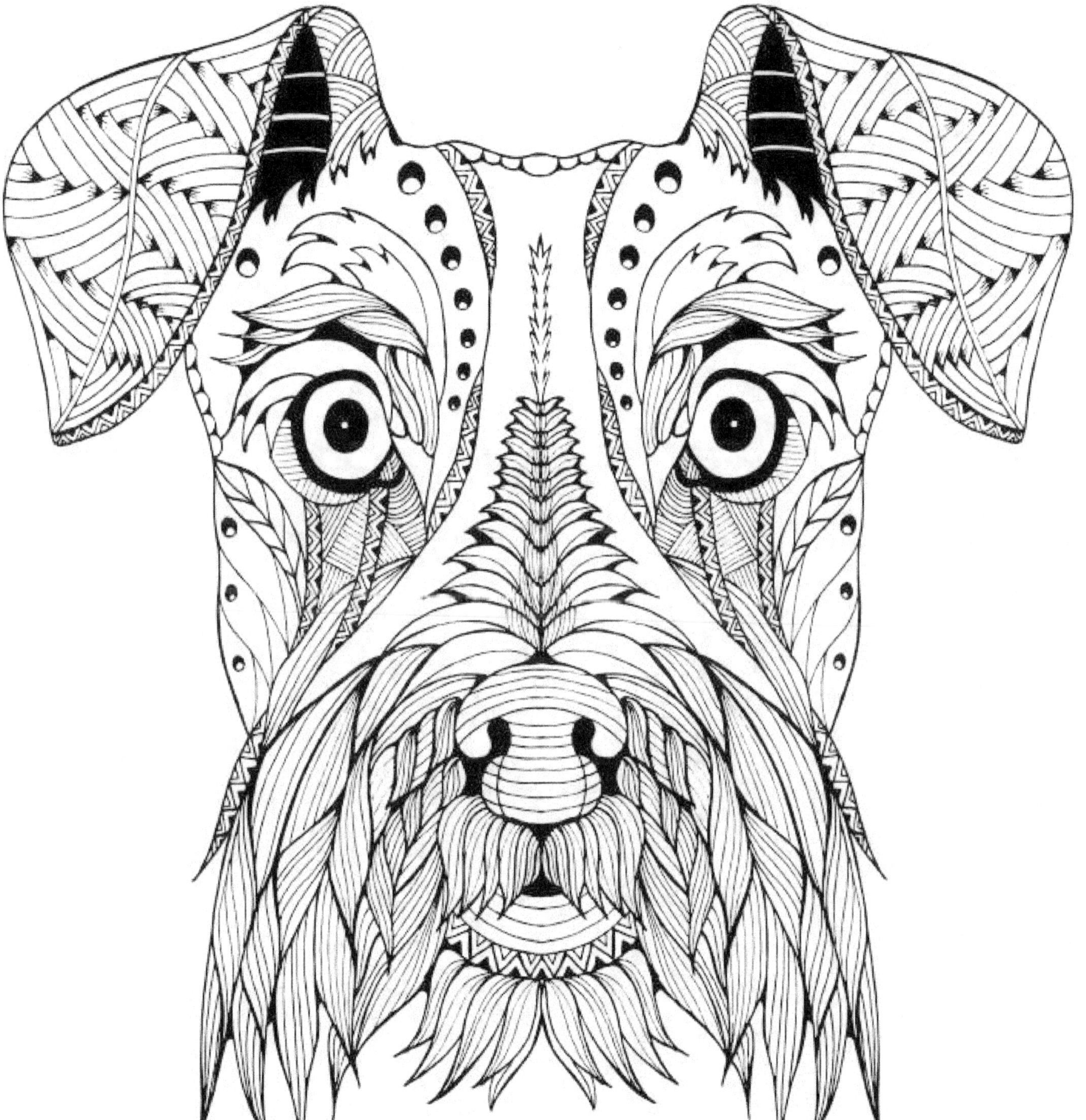

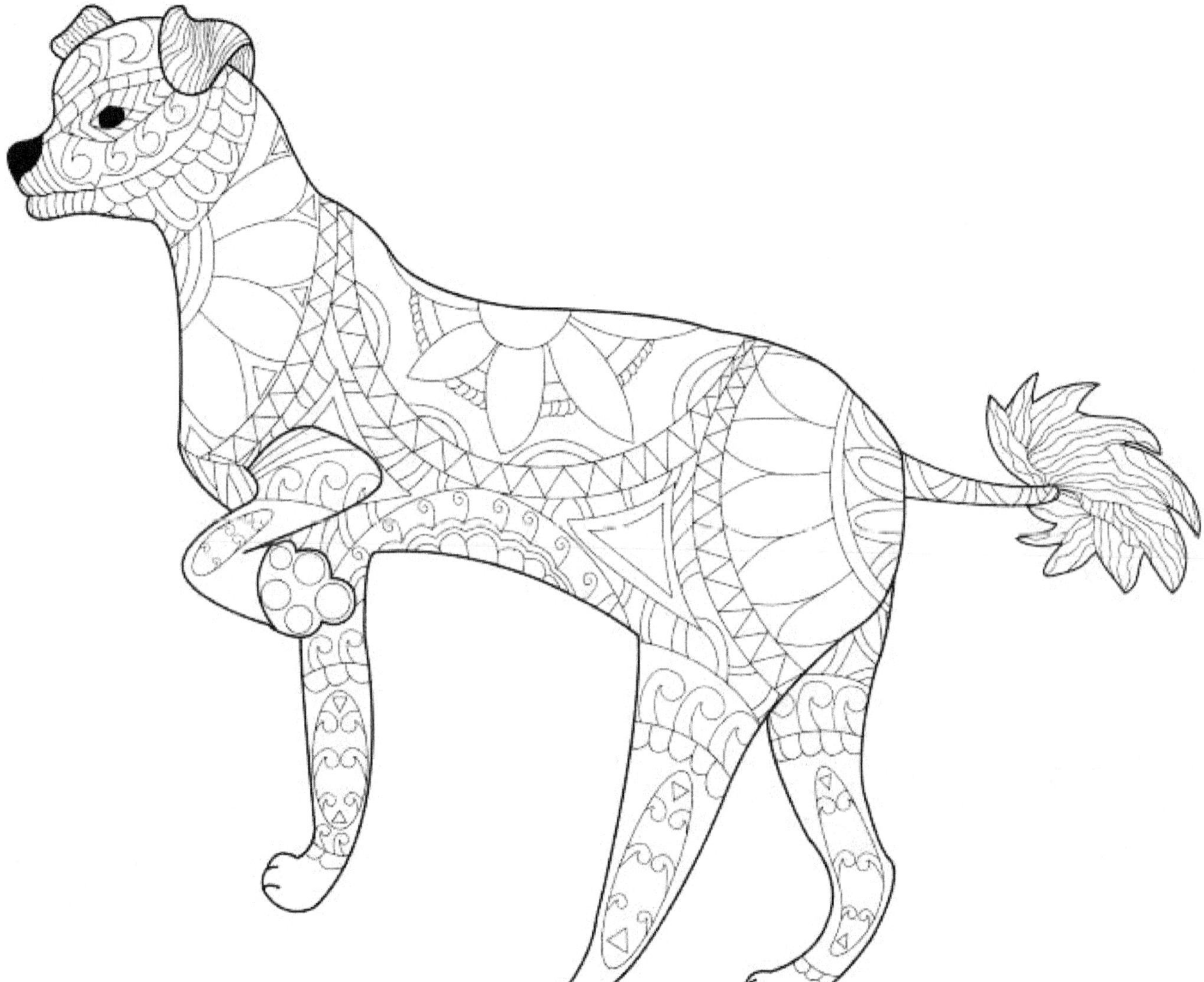

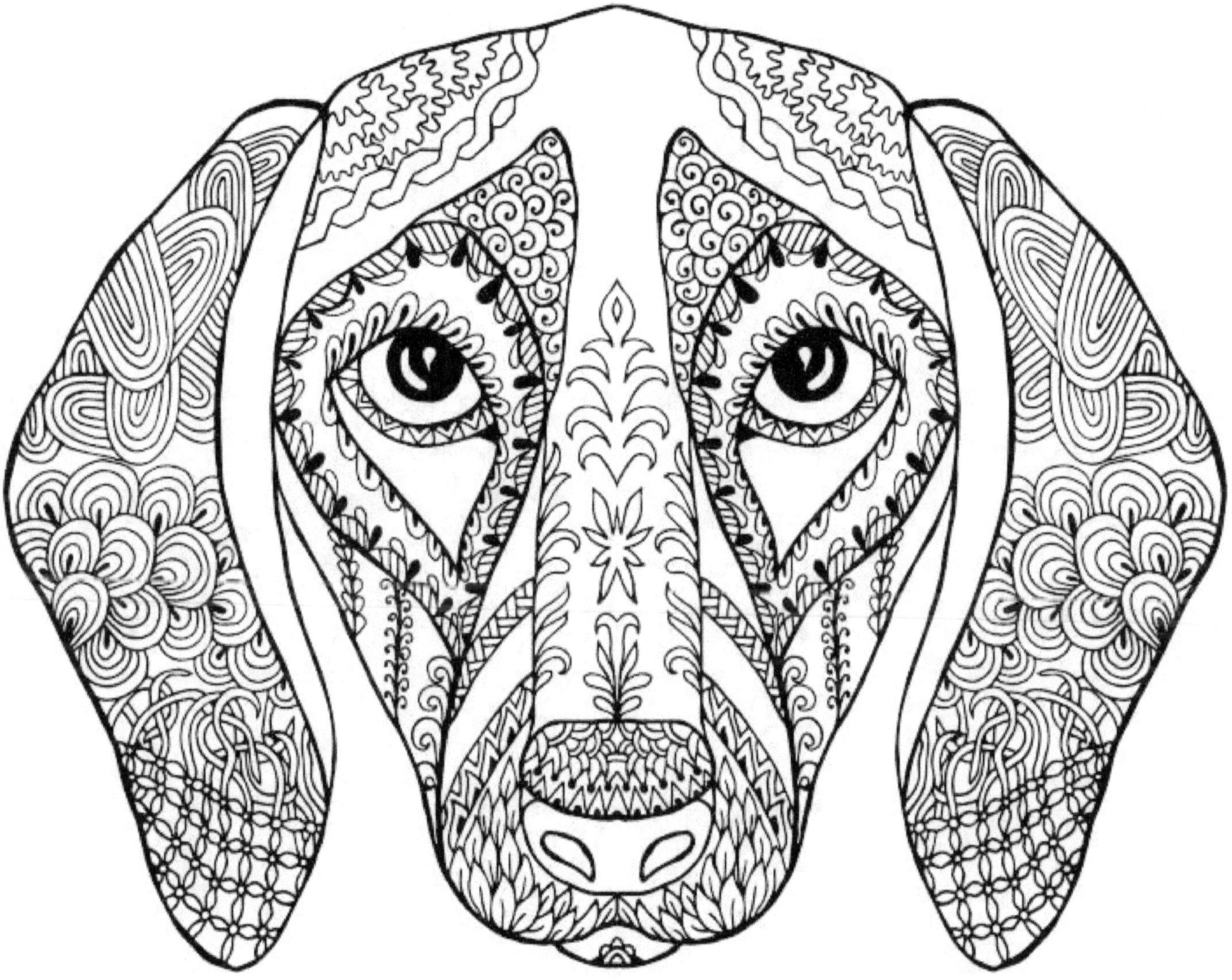

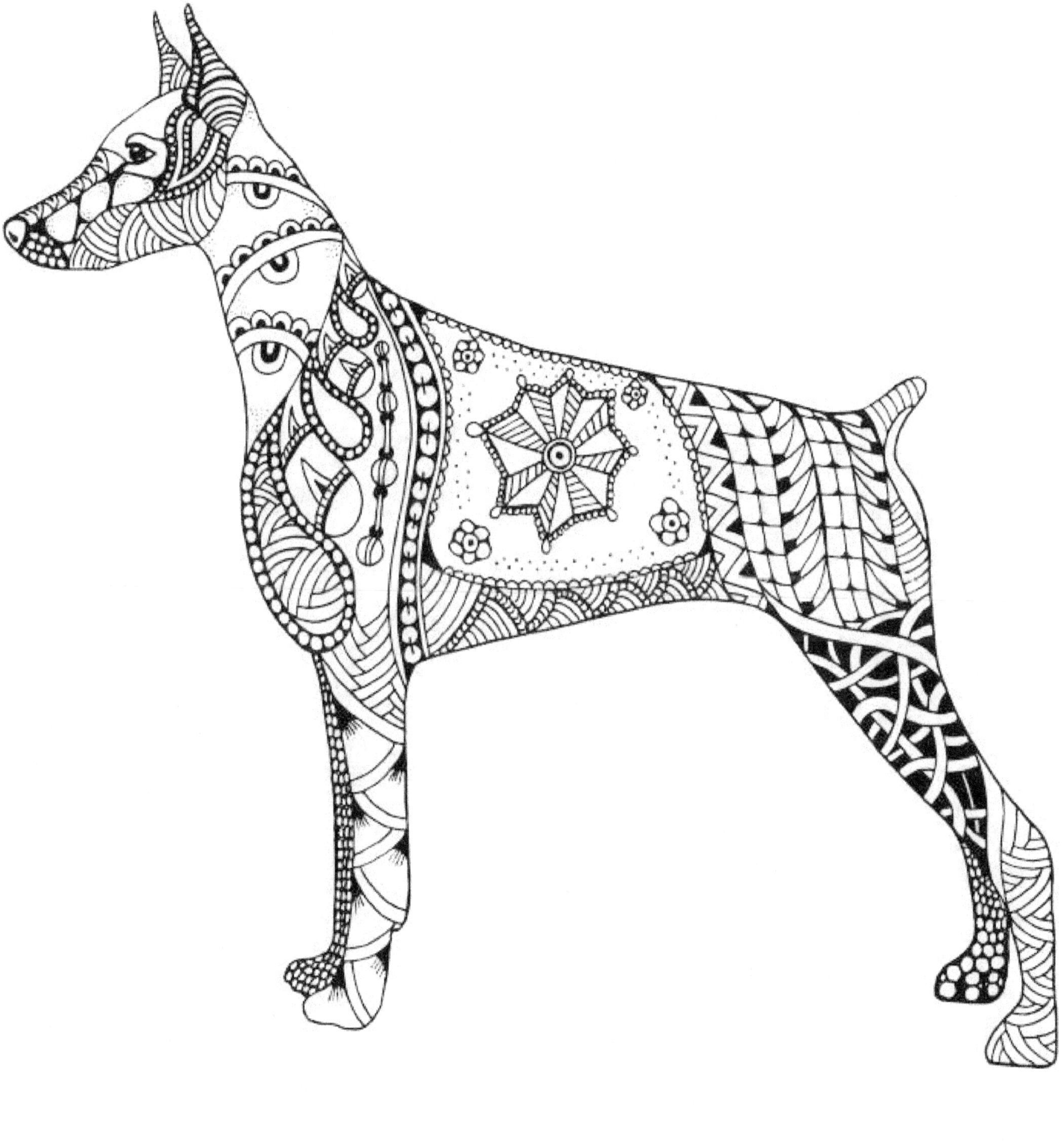

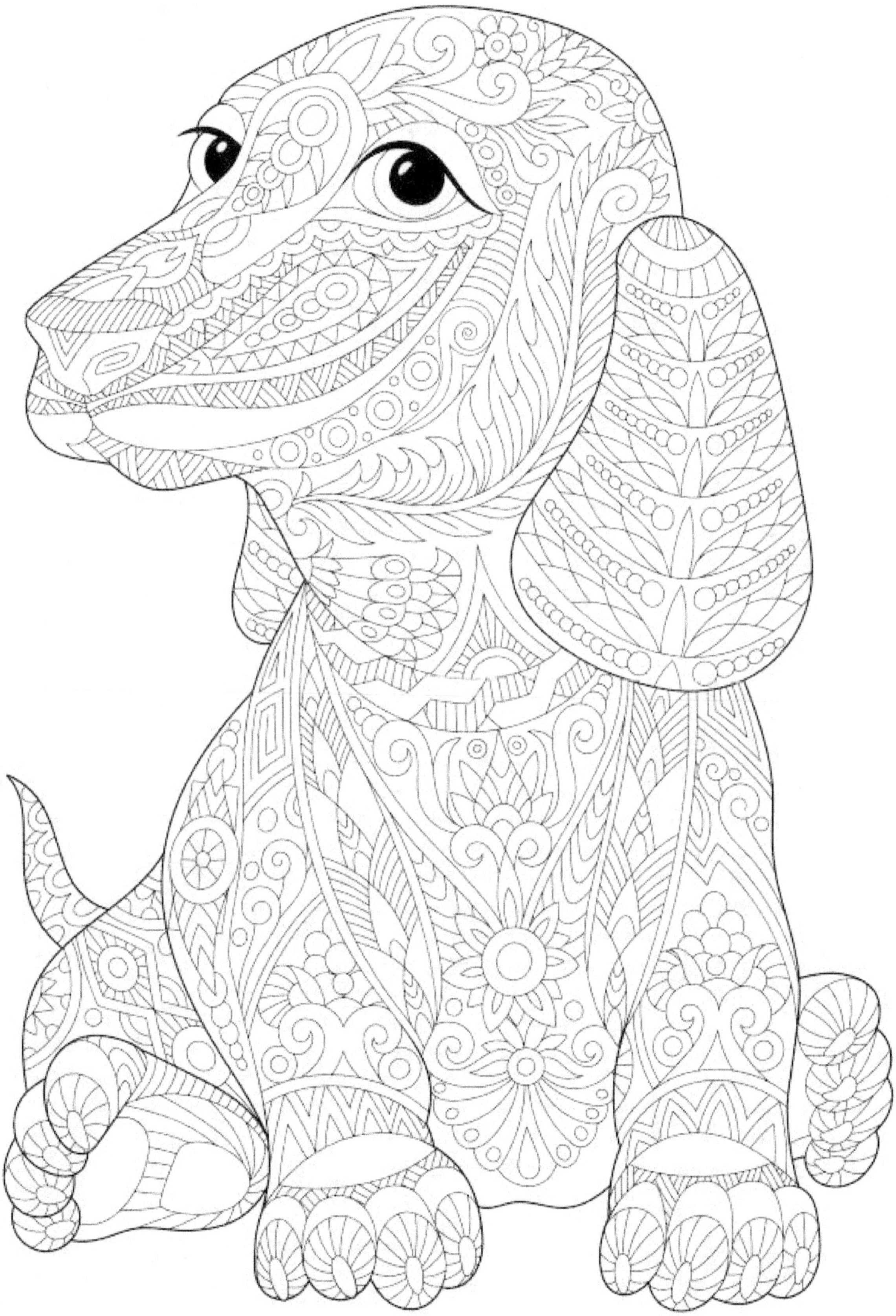

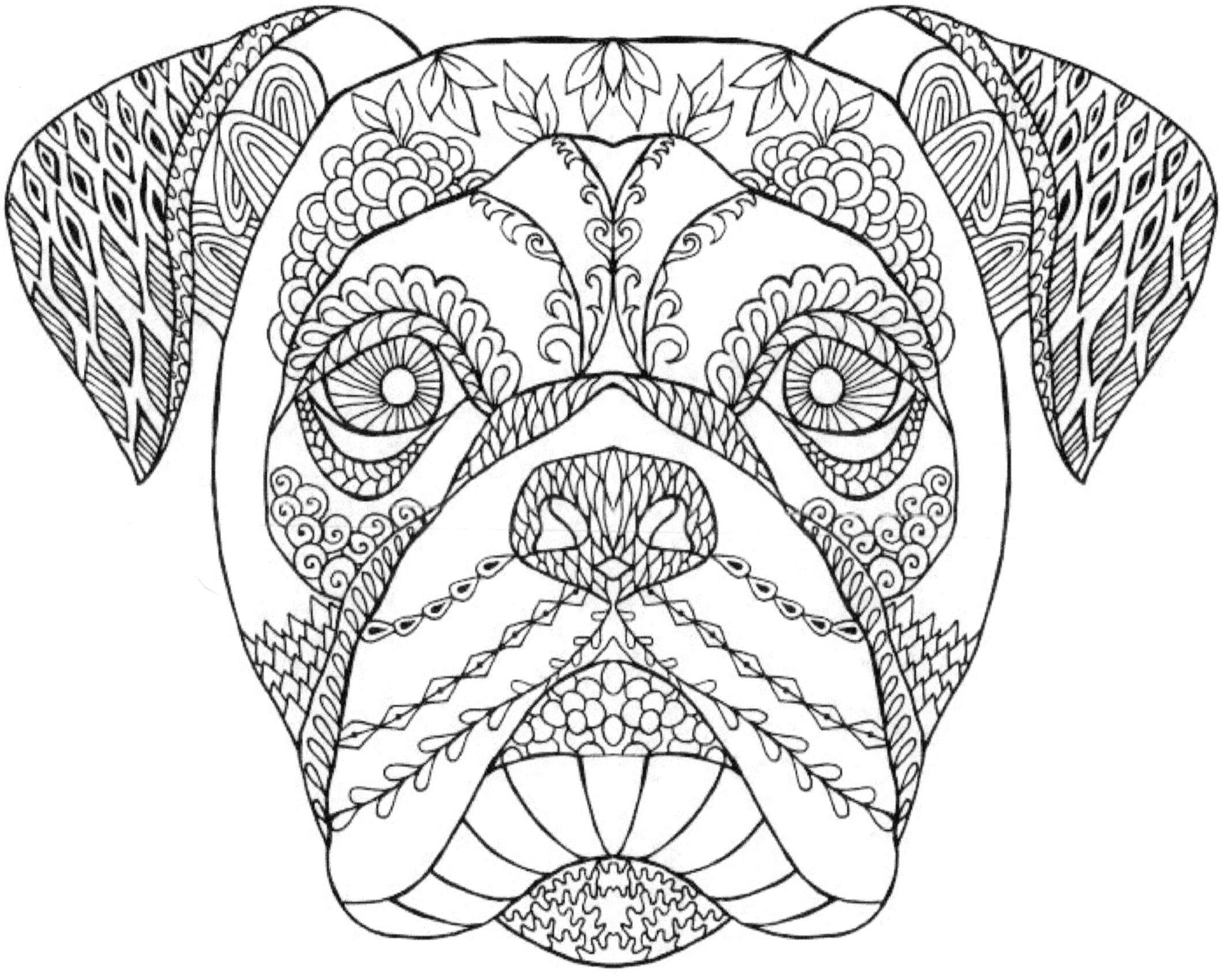

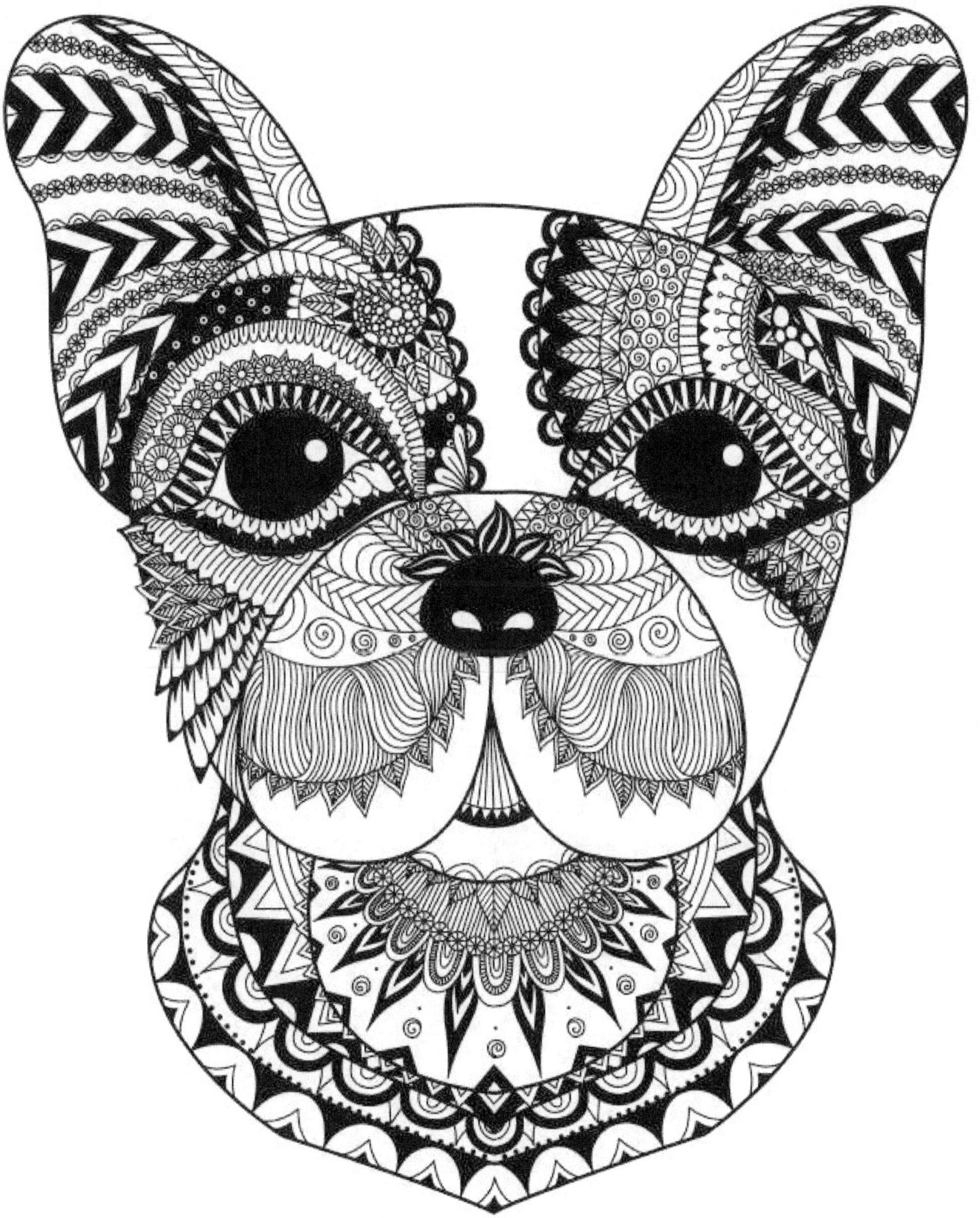

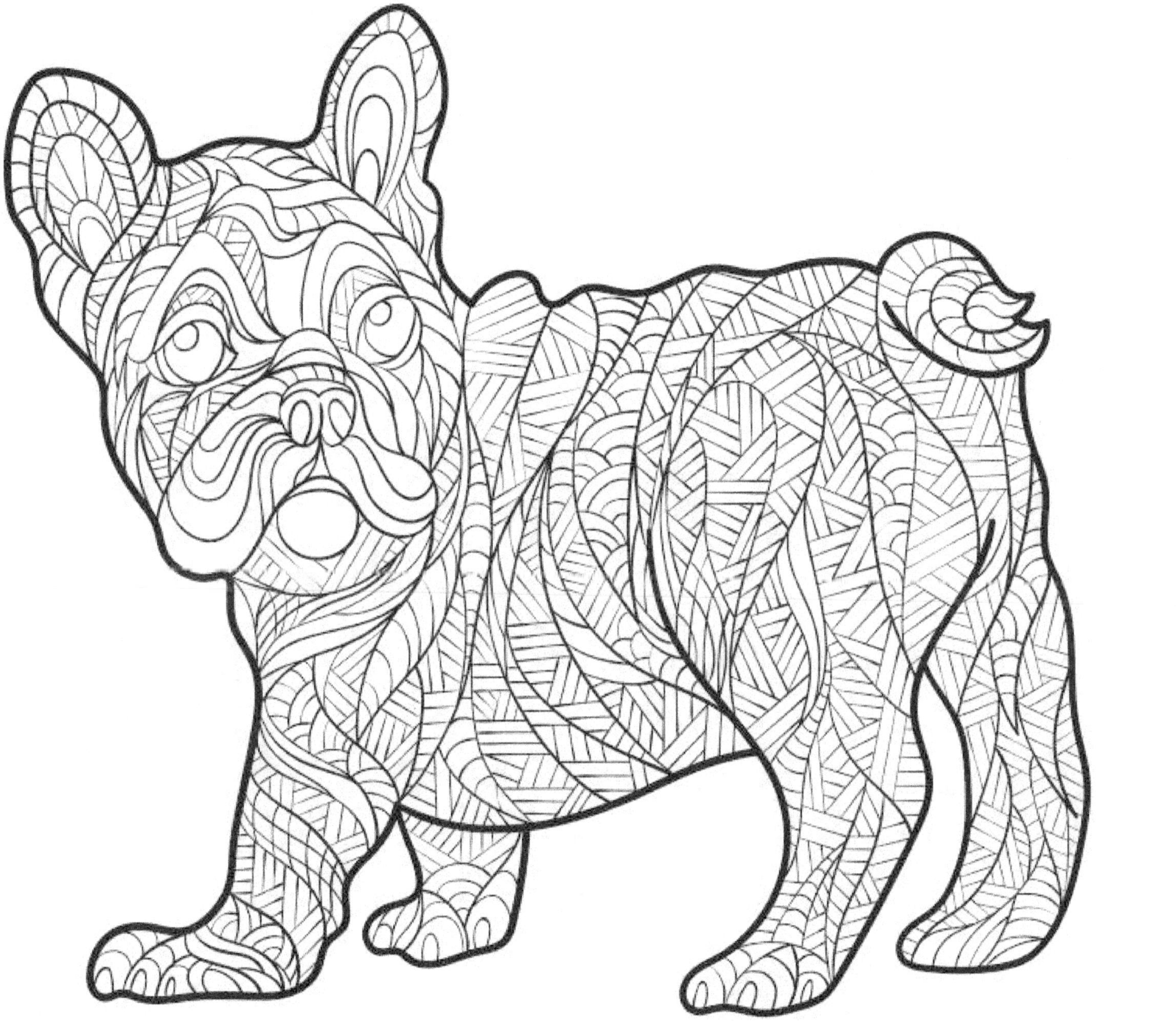

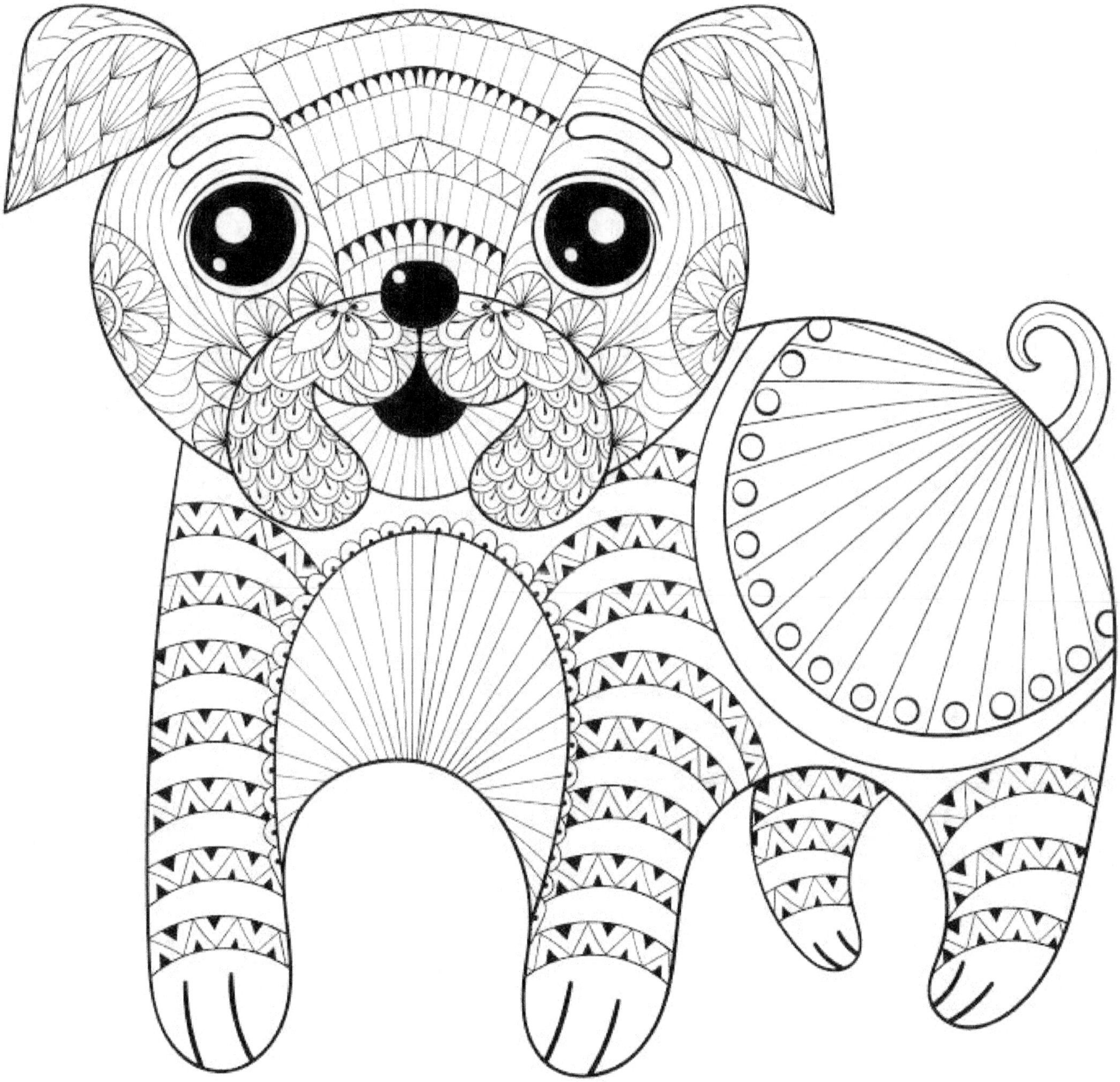

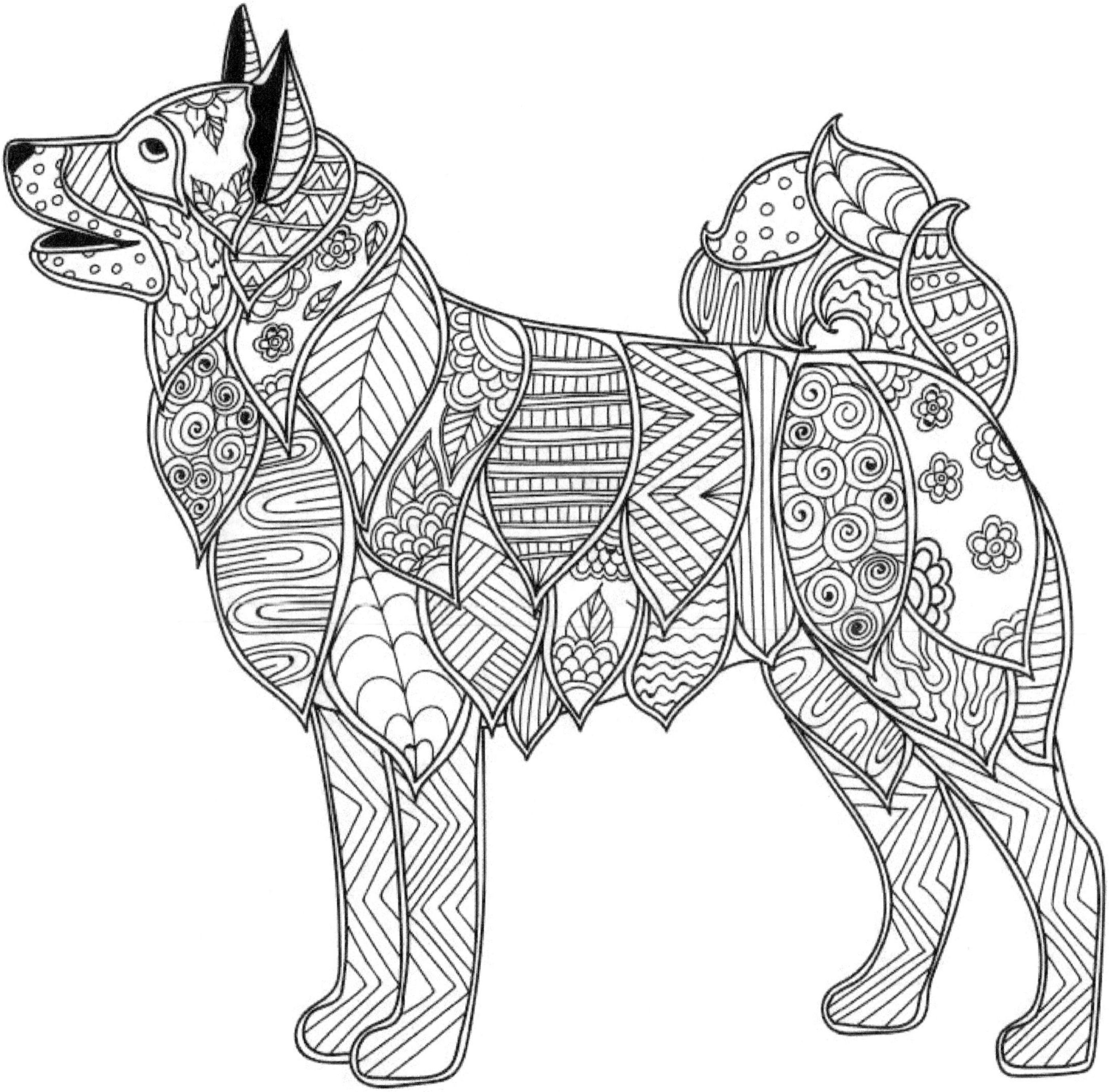

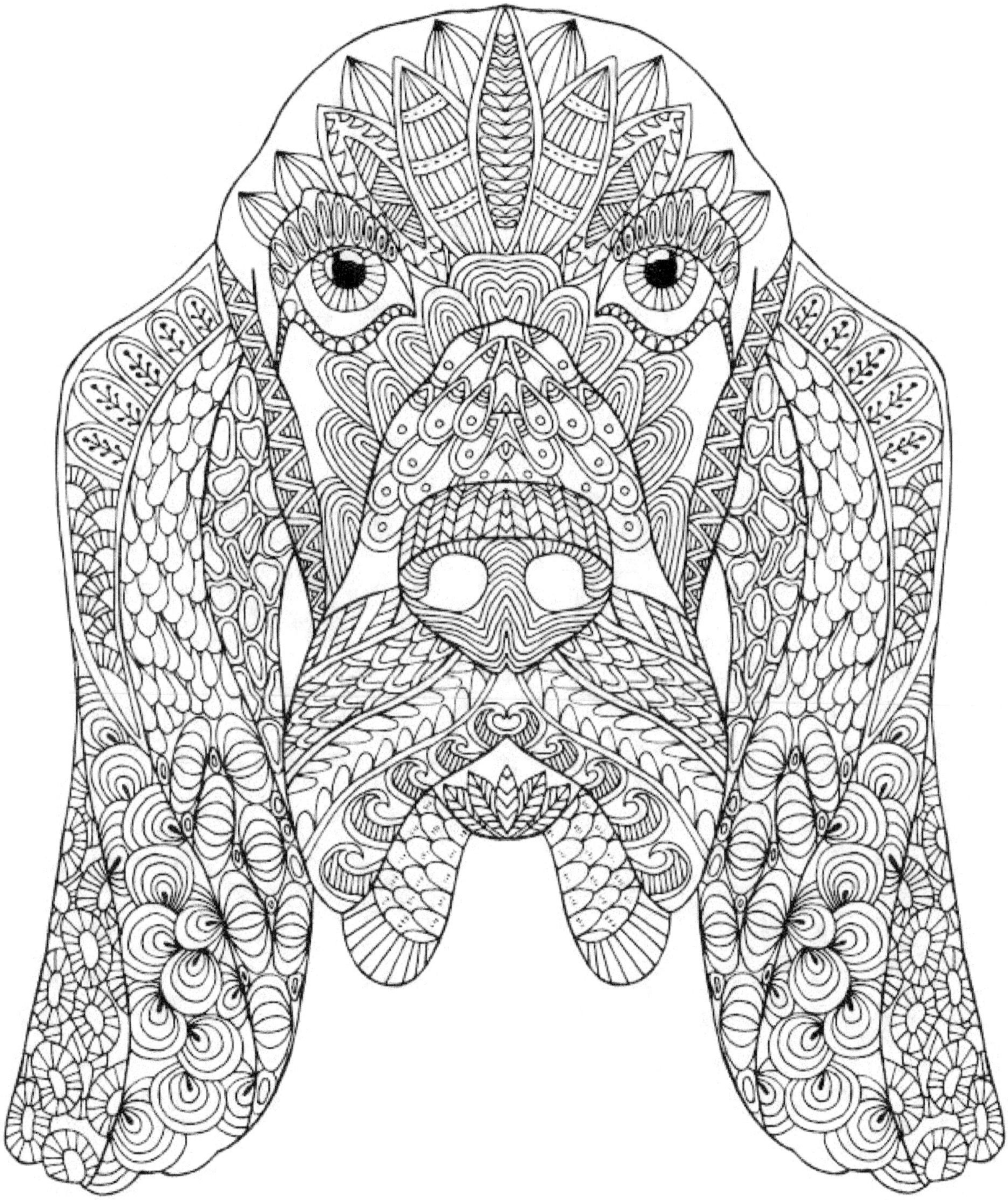

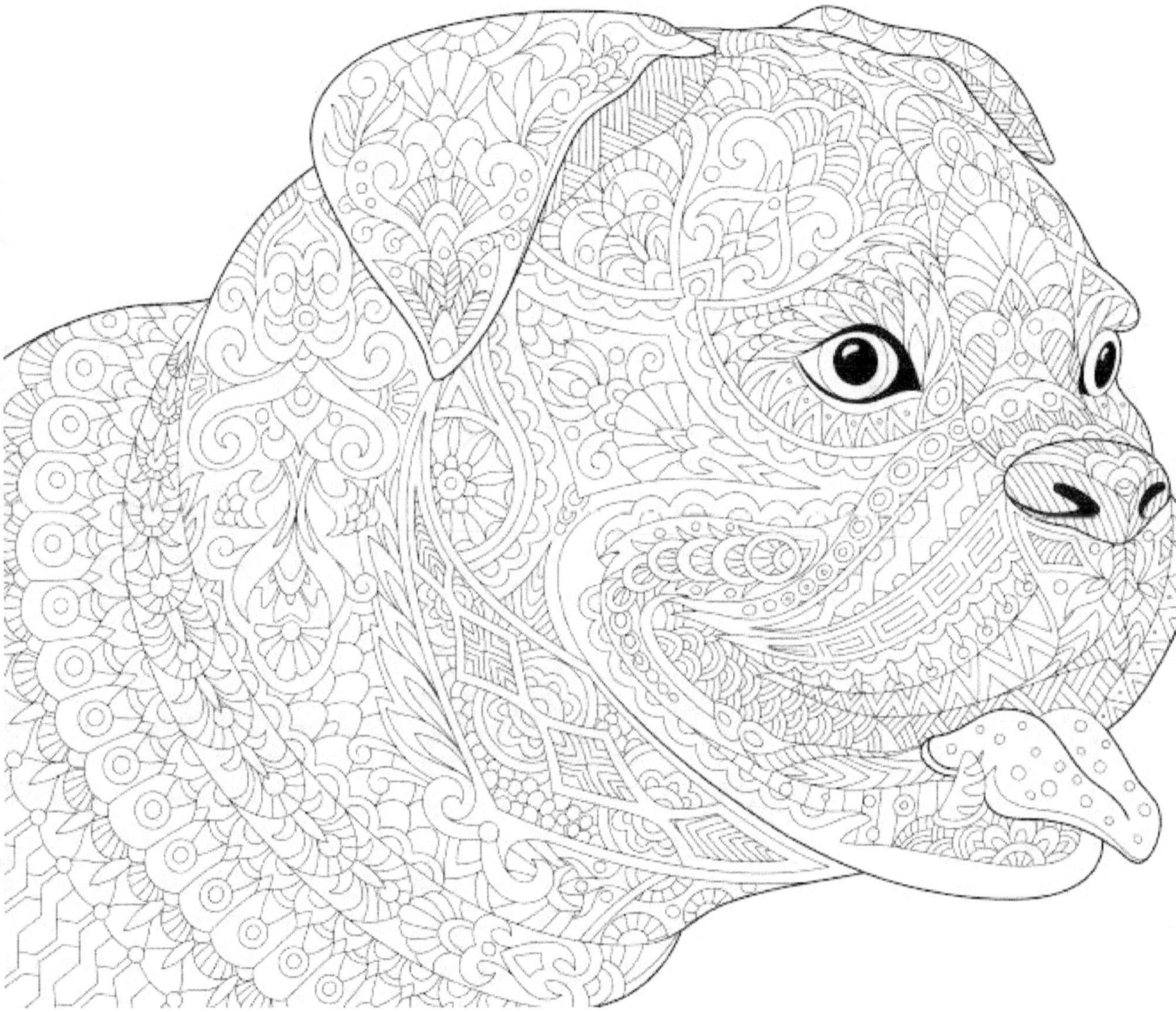

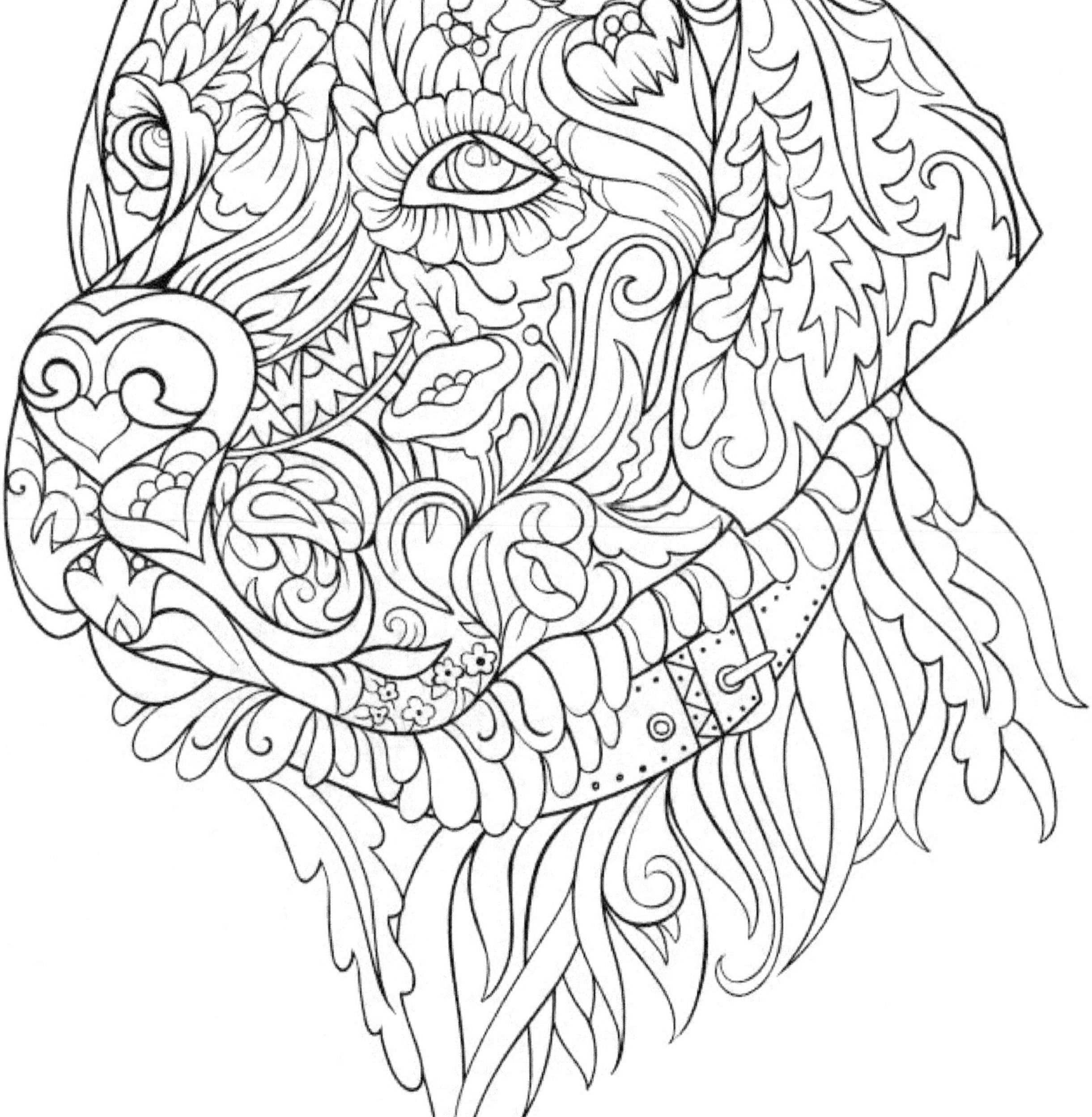

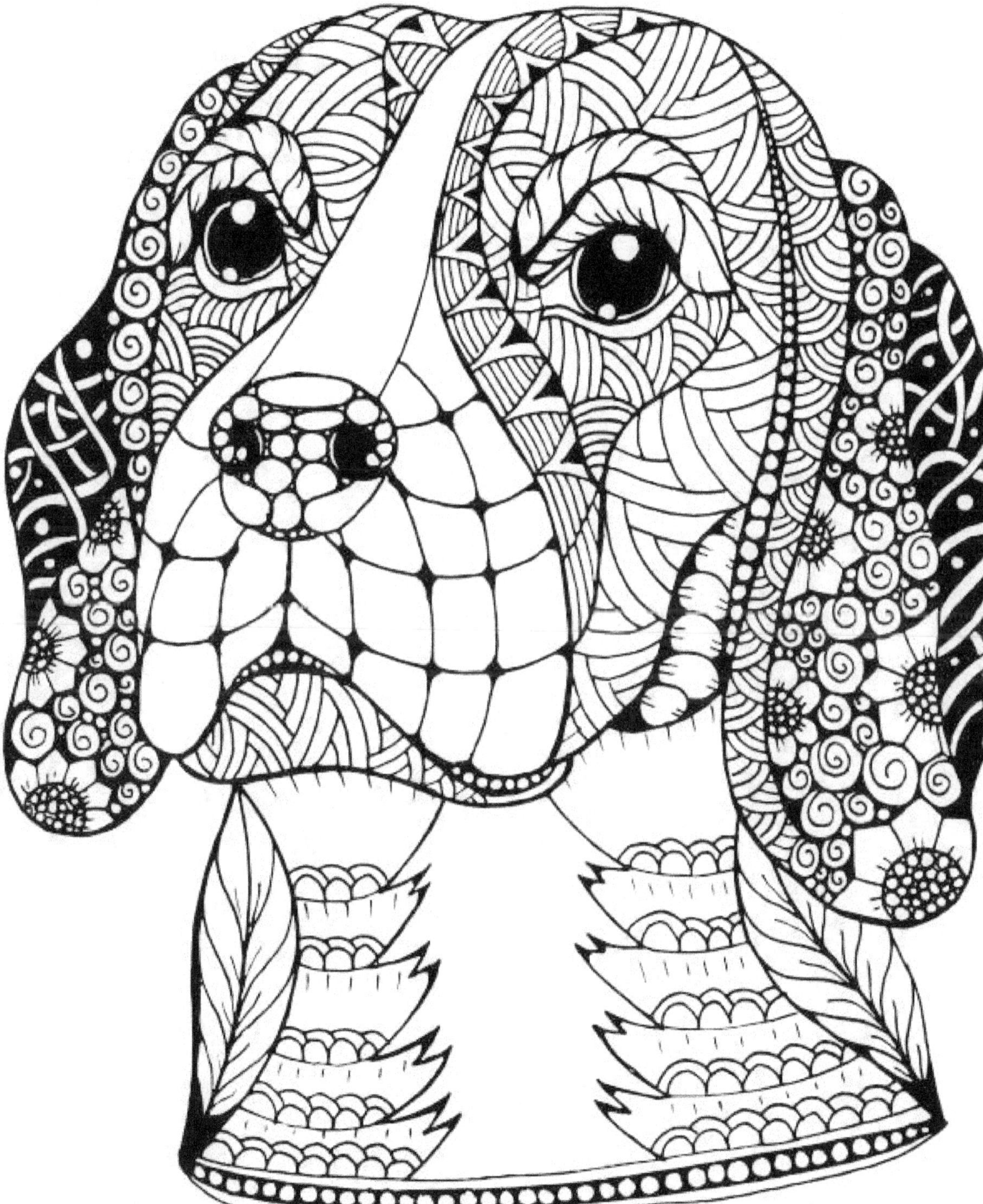

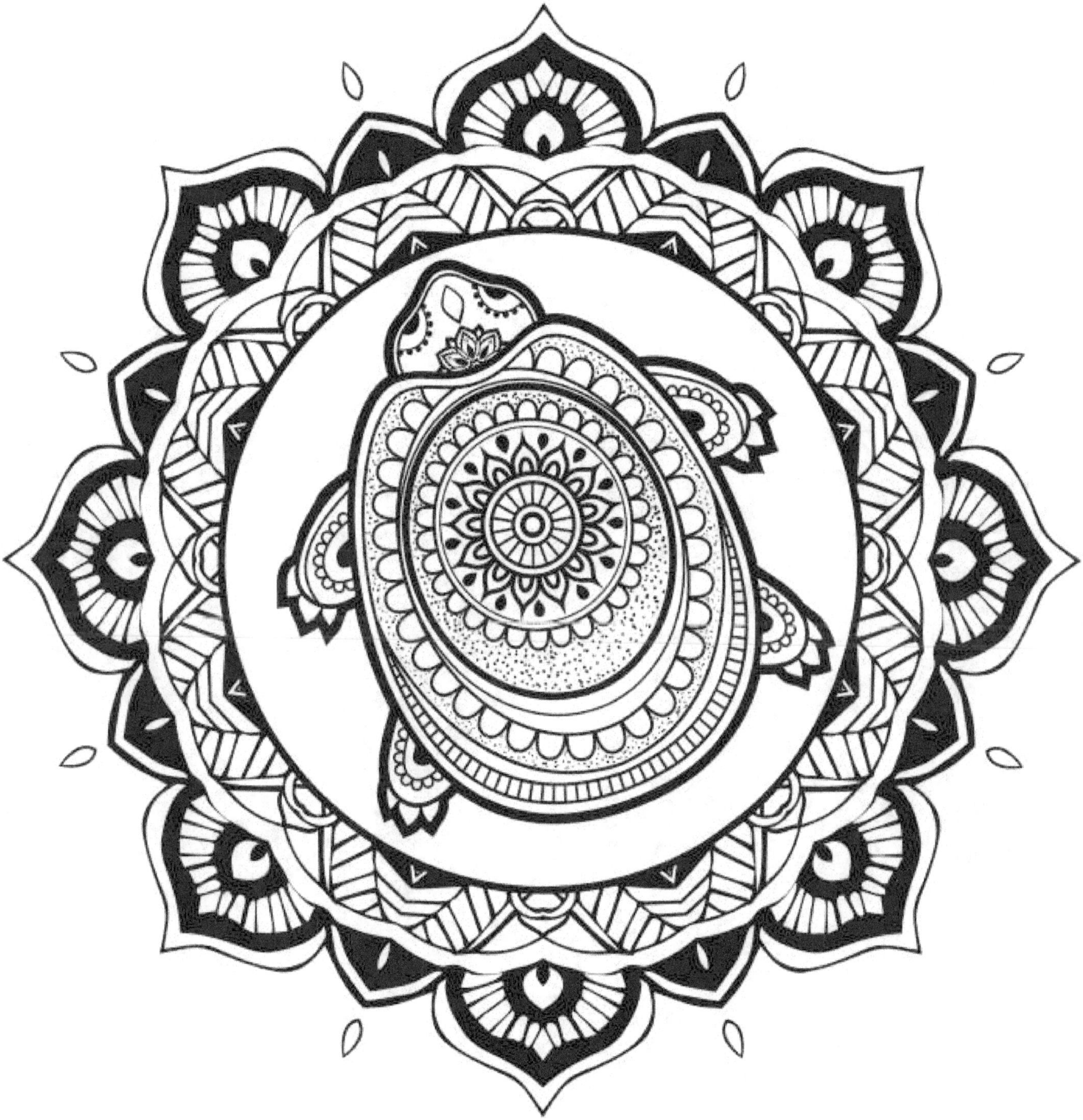

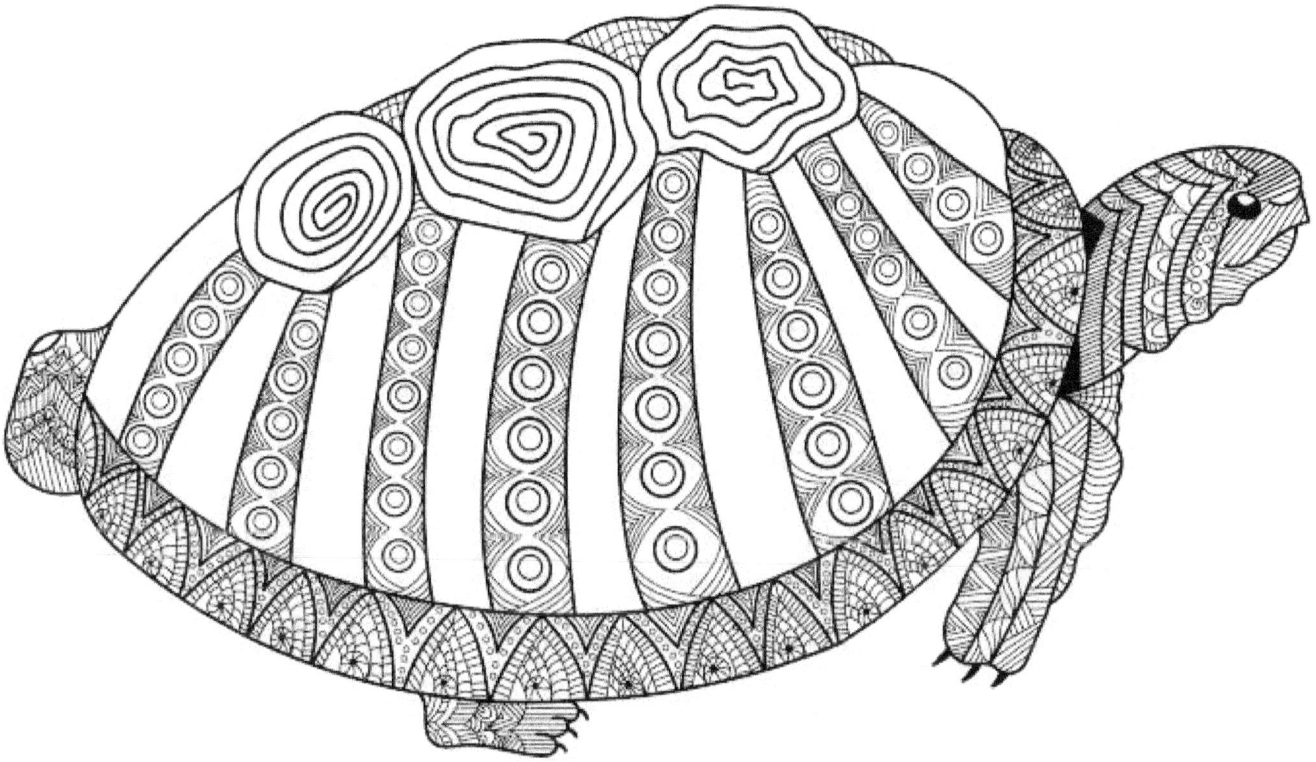

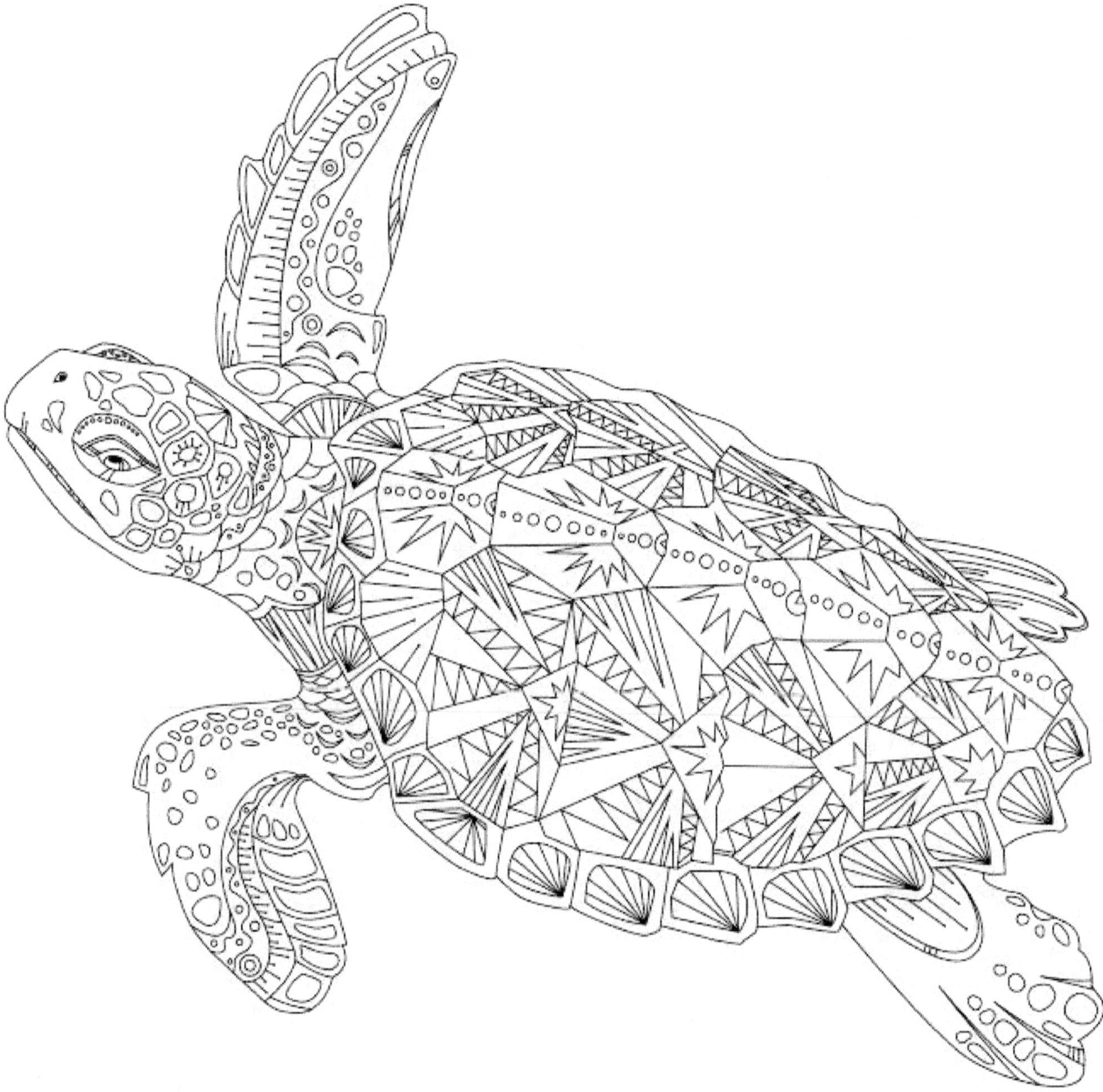

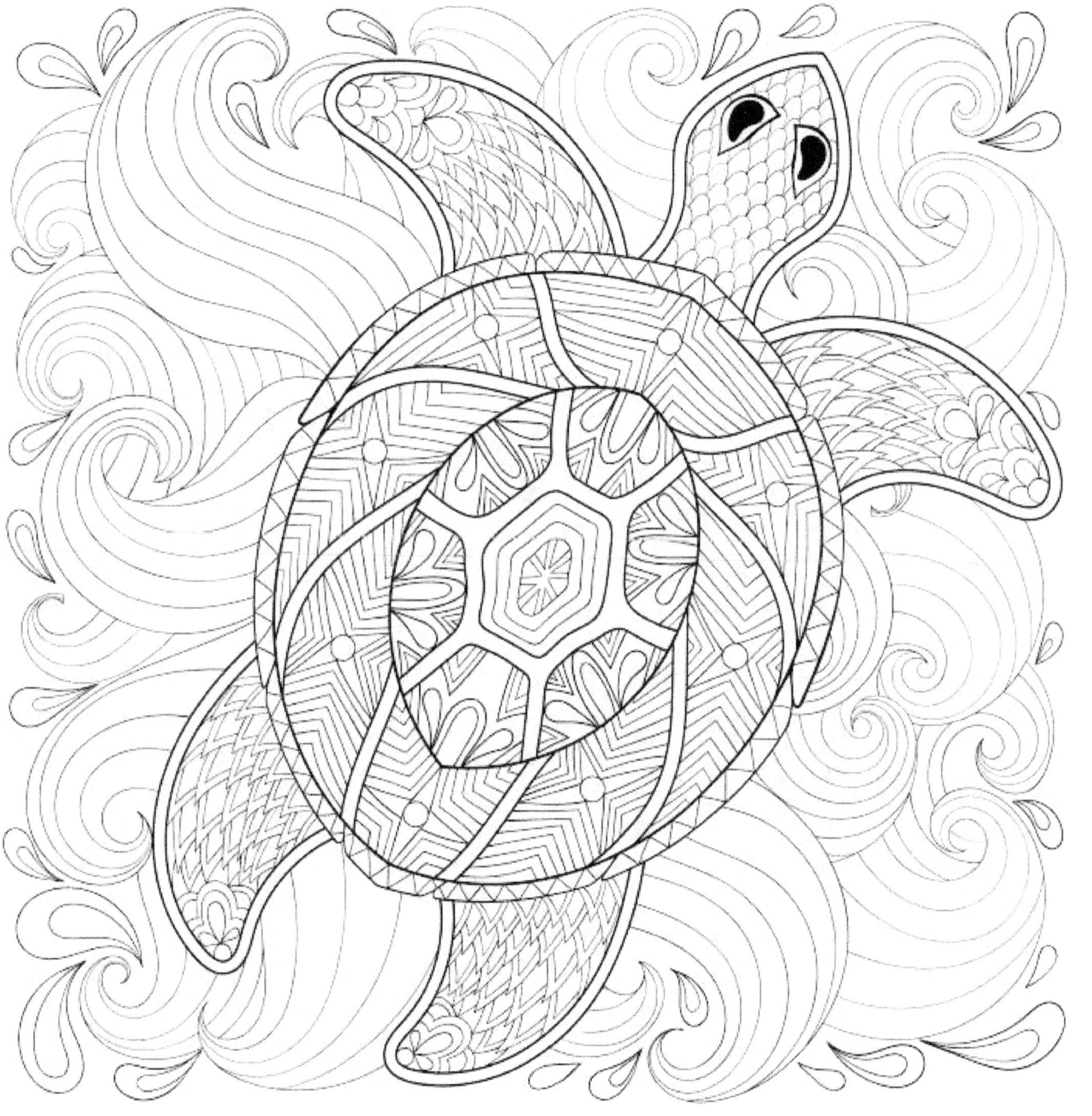

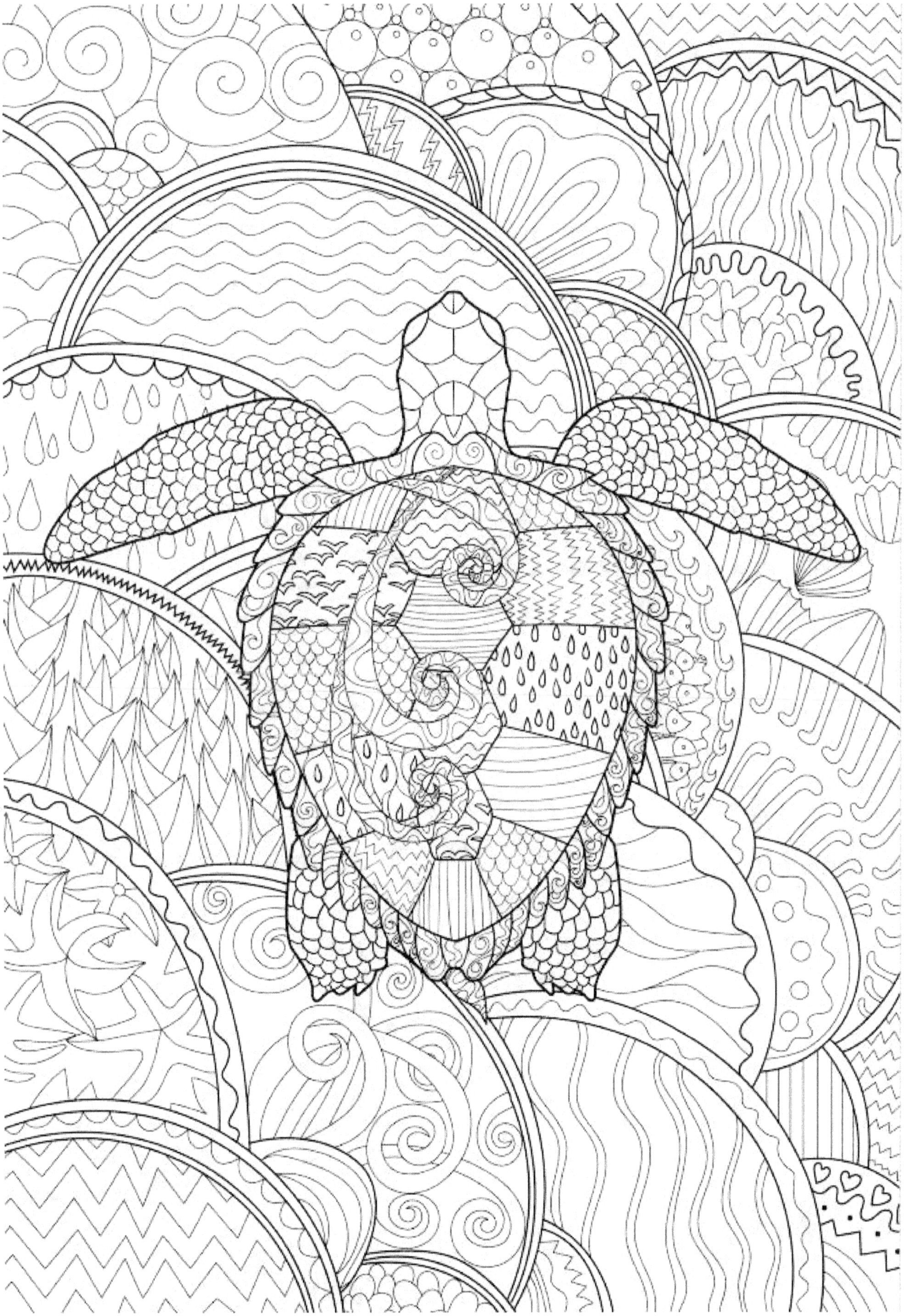

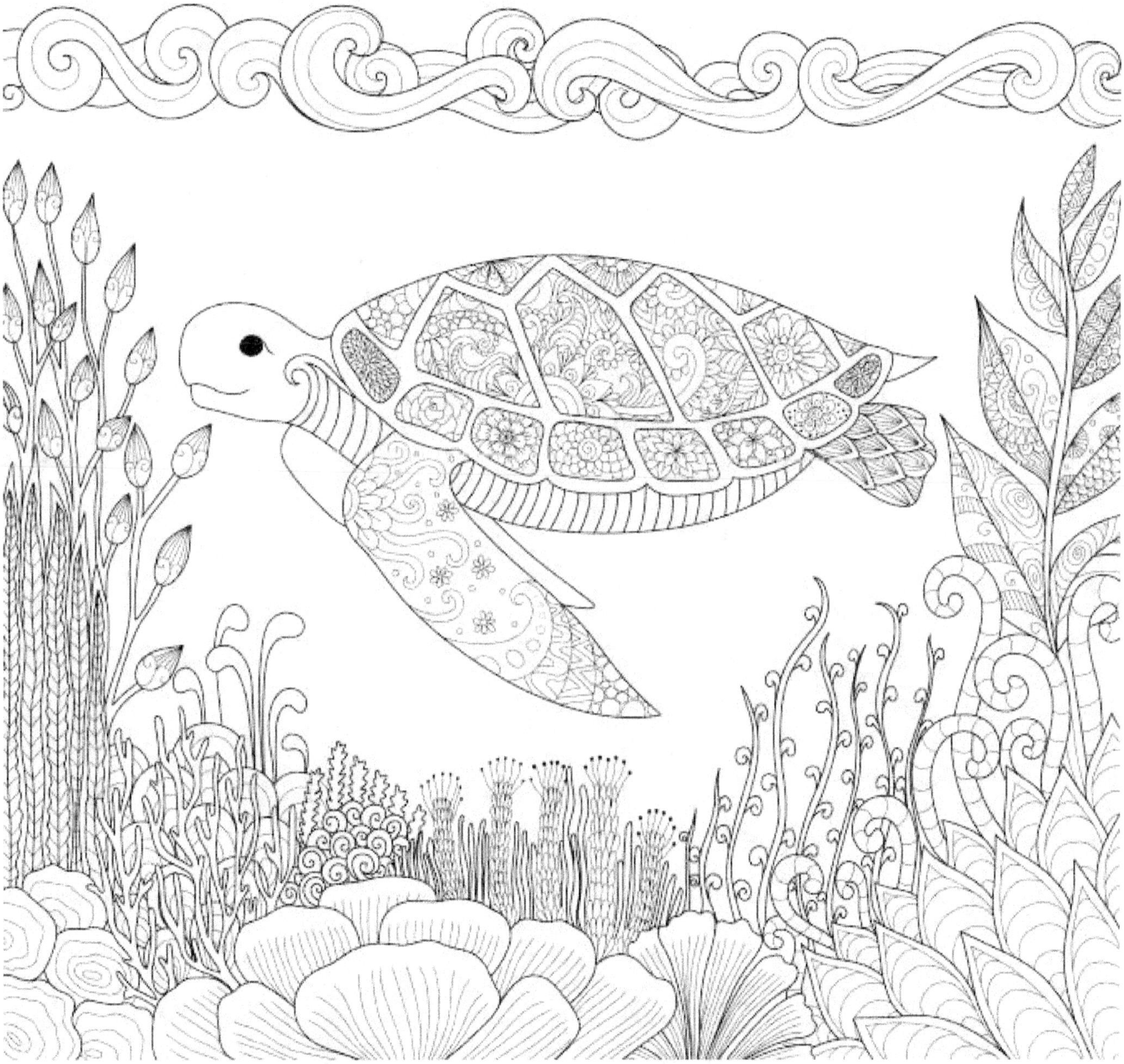

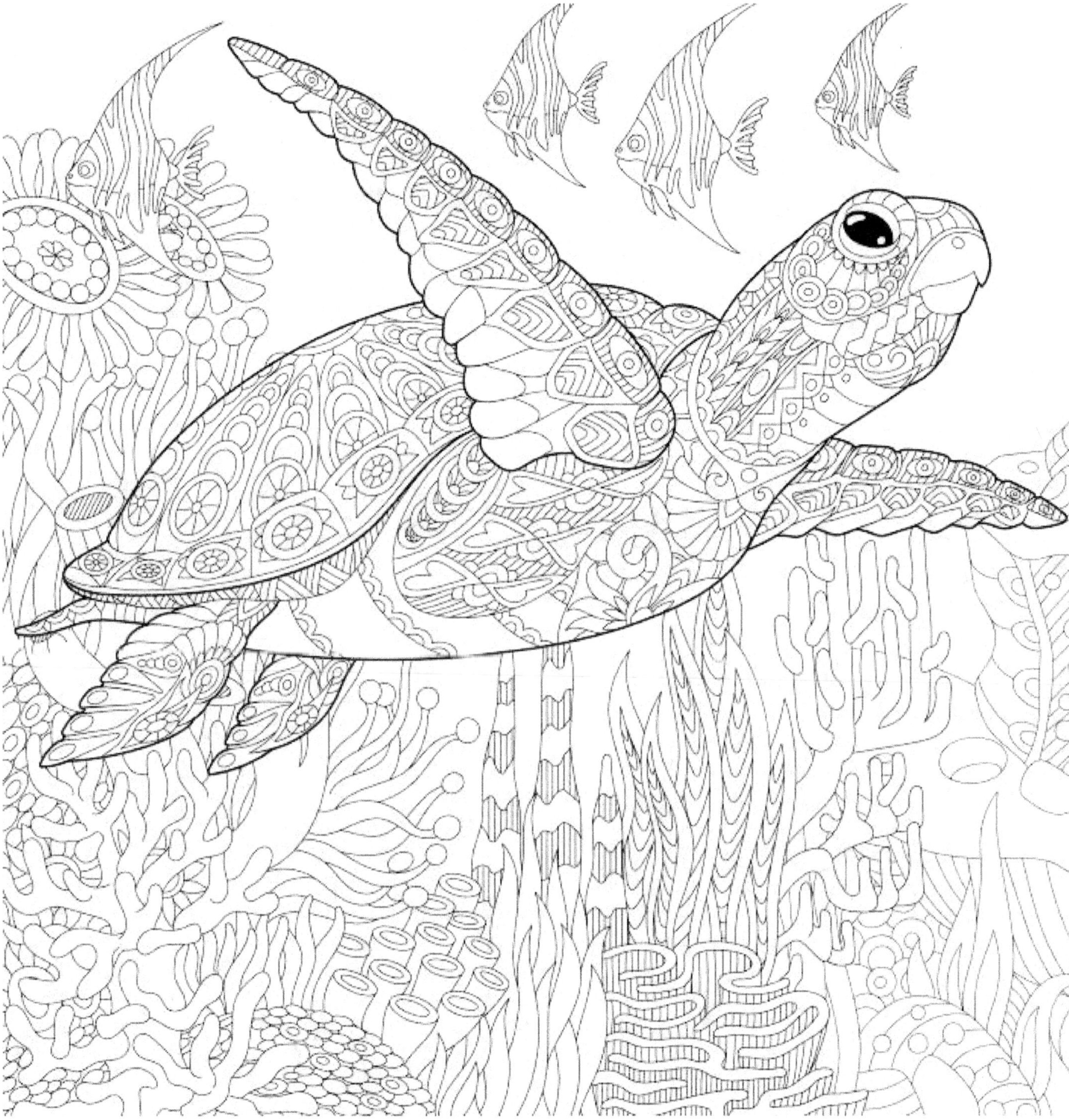

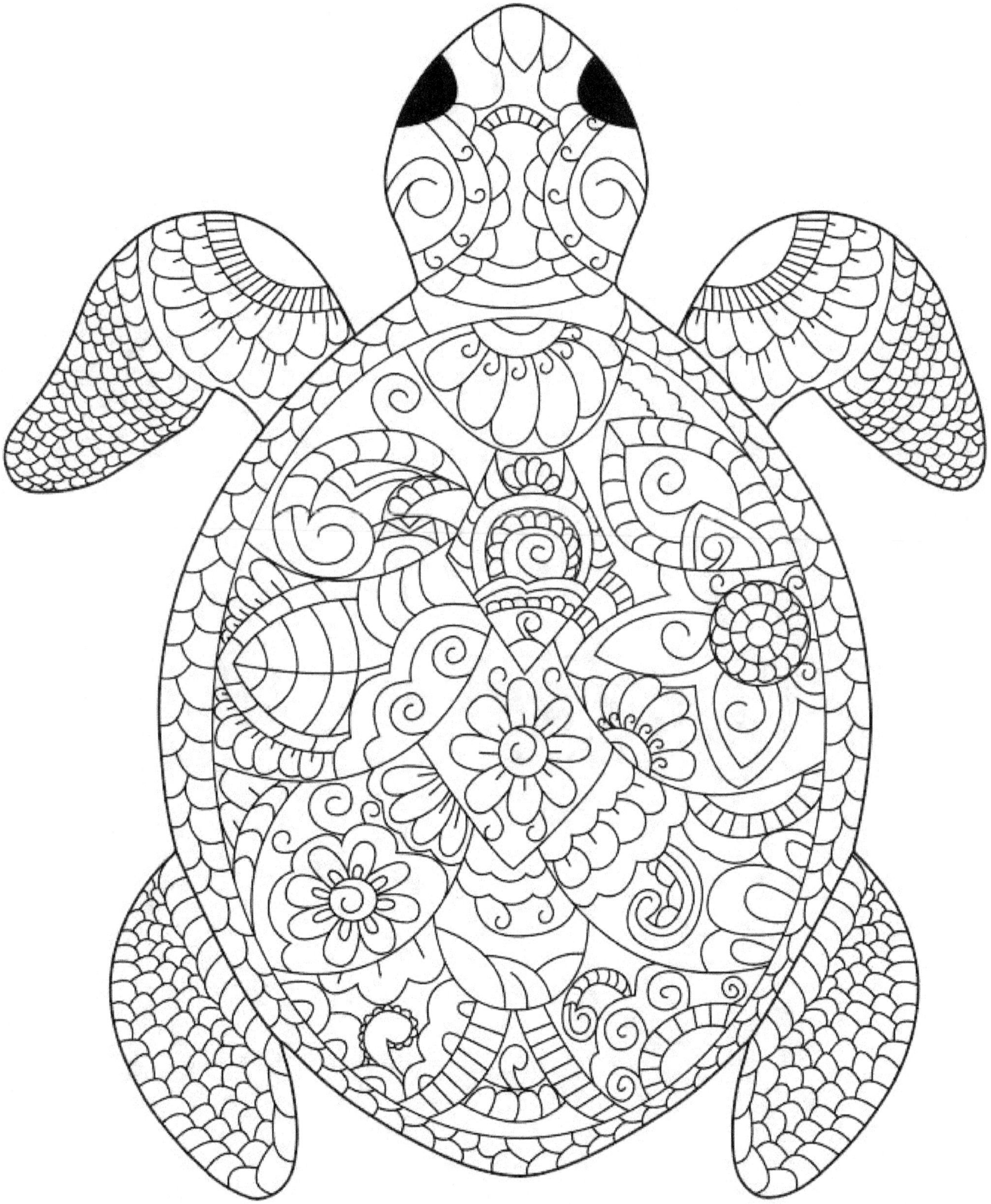

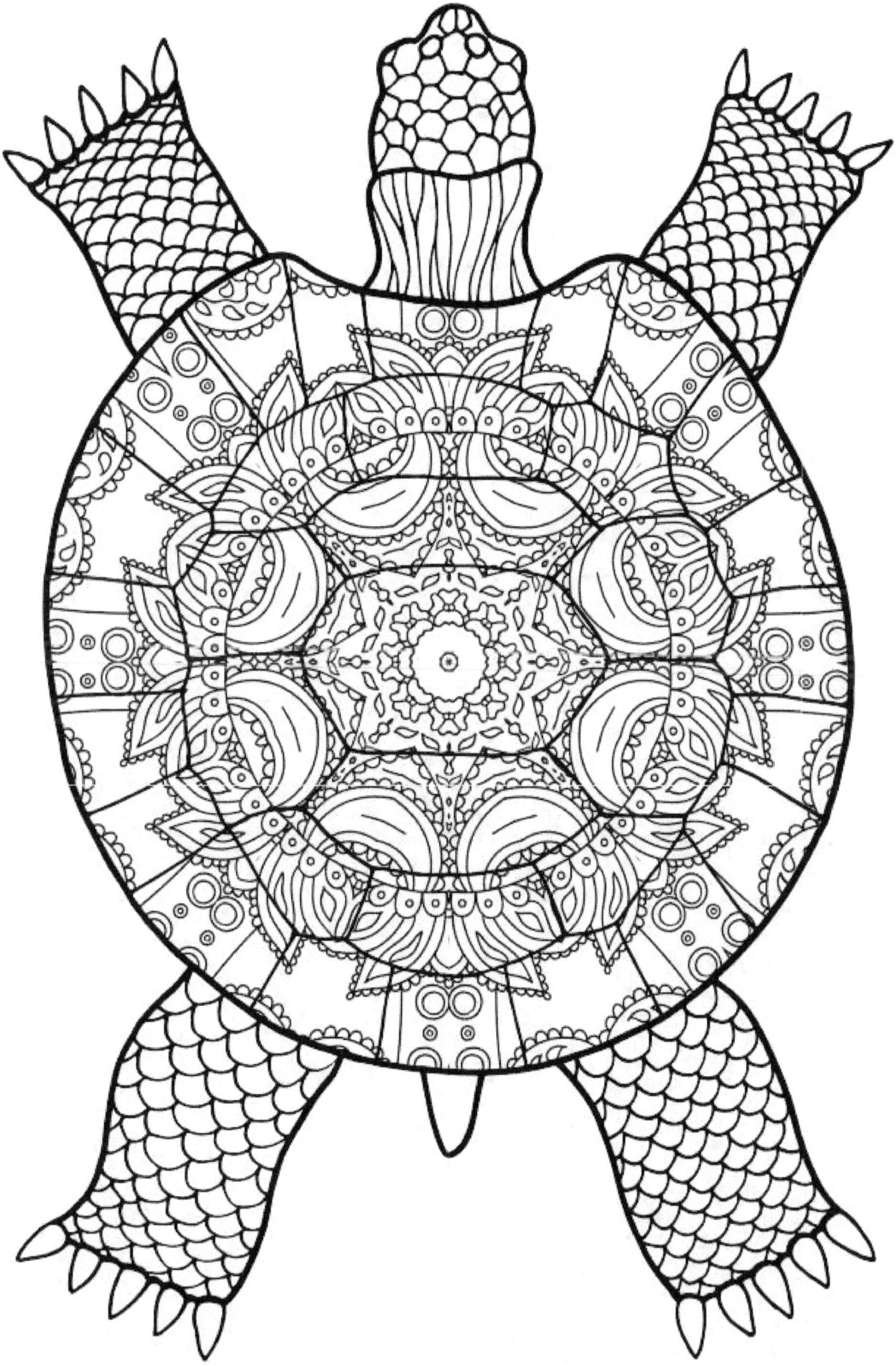

www.ingramcontent.com/pod-product-compliance
Lightning Source LLC
Chambersburg PA
CBHW081214170526
45165CB00009B/2821
* 9 7 8 1 5 4 7 1 4 3 2 9 0 *